Spanish-American Folktales

Spanish-American Folktales

"Short on verbiage and long in wisdom, the illustrated tales will appeal both to child and adult, with their humor, cleverness, wit and wry twists which mirror a real cultural tradition."

—**Mary M. Fisher,** *The North San Antonio Times*

"This collection is the product of a love affair with the oral tale that has lasted over a score of years."

—**John. O. West,** *Mid-America Folklore*

"Starting to read these stories is like eating potato chips, you can't stop yourself from just one more until you have finished the entire book."

—**Marcia Muth,** *(New Mexico) Enchantment*

Spanish-American Folktales

The practical wisdom of Spanish-Americans in 28 eloquent and simple stories.

Teresa Pijoan de Van Etten

August House Publishers, Inc.

L I T T L E   R O C K

Printed in the United States of America

10 9 8 7 6 5 4 3 2

LIBRARY OF CONGRESS CATALOGING-IN-PUBLICATION DATA

Van Etten, Teresa Pijoan
Spanish-American Folktales / Teresa Pijoan Van Etten. — 1st ed.
    p. cm.
    ISBN 0-87483-155-5 (alk. paper) : $9.95
1. Spanish Americans—New Mexico—Folklore. 2. Tales—New Mexico
        I. Title.

GR111.S65V36 1990
398.2'089'680789—dc20   90-42303

First Edition, 1990

Executive: Ted Parkhurst
Project editor: Judith Faust
Cover design and illustrations: Wendell E. Hall
Typography: Lettergraphics, Memphis

PUBLISHERS

AUGUST HOUSE, INC.

LITTLE ROCK

To my brother
señor Olivario Pijoan

Acknowledgments

The translations are my own, with support from señor Tomás Van Etten, el señor profesor Orlando Vigil, Kathleen Valencia, Donnie Nelson, Phillip Rivera, Jessica Arquero, Robert Trujillo, Trisha Moquino, Shaun Roman, Pedro Mariscal, Bernadette Romero, Kurt Stueber, Ruben Lucero, Ernie Gutierrez, Stephanie Archibeque, Shirley Estrada, Gabriel Archibeque, Rosa Cervantes, Olivia Corie, Theron Pecos, Theresa Eustace, Ruben Candelaria, Jeremy Myers and Vidal.

Preface

You are important. What you feel inside, what you know, the story that you hold within you is important for all of you, and your life is important.

New Mexico holds the wealth of many cultures, many stories, and many different traditions. The winds of time bring change. The seasons grow old and pass. Still, with each season comes the memory of what has gone before, and we learn to remember.

Each year, we must herd sheep along the tall mesas. When the day is done, and it is quiet once more, our fires make a little light under the night sky. People come to the fires to share. The day's trials are told with both humor and gravity. Stories remembered from long ago are told, as well. Once, after we had been many nights out on the mesa, I began to read from a book. The first night on the mesa, there had been fourteen sheepherders about the fire, but when the third chapter of that old library book was read on the twelfth night, there were twenty-eight faces silently listening. In the morning, only fourteen stood in line for breakfast.

The power of the story brings life to the night fires. The power of sharing brings people together.

I was born in Española, New Mexico—a town with its own story, a town whose name comes from a tale of a beautiful Spanish woman. I was raised on the San Juan Pueblo Indian Reservation by my father, who was from Barcelona, Spain, and my mother, who was from New York City. They were busy being doctor, teacher, farmers, drivers, and landowners. My three brothers and I were raised by many—and at times by other families. The wealth of stories, languages, traditions, and memories have kept us separate and together through all of our lives.

I learned to appreciate the power of the story, and the faces behind the stories. Being short on money did not mean that one was poor. Having a bad story was poverty. Having no story at all was beyond poverty, it was humiliation. We learned that everyone has the power of imagination and creativity, and the wealth and knowledge of laughter, sadness, or love to share.

We need stories because they hold the power of feeling and life. The stories I heard and told at home are the same stories I've shared from California to New York. Many have forgotten the power of stories. Many have forgotten to feel—don't know that it is still all right to feel.

When I tell stories, I bring the audience up with me to participate as characters in the stories, for the stories aren't about the teller, they're about the characters with whom we can all identify. People from the audience participate beside each other, and me, and the tale itself. When the story is over and we have touched, we are united in the empathy of the feelings portrayed. There is no stronger bond than that of sharing feelings. And we can do it though stories any time.

The doctor's office is full of stories. The grocery store line is a place where everyone shares tales and gossip. Life is as rich as the land's own colors. There is always the wealth of stories.

These stories are from the land and people of New Mexico. Once you have read them, some of them may become a part of you, and you can tell them your way. They will grow, taking on the color of your traditions, land, and memories. They will join your stories. Your stories are important.

May the power of your story always be your wealth.

Life is full, life is rich,

Teresa Pijoan de Van Etten

Contents

Leaf Monster

Up north near Guachepangue, there lived a fine fat coyote who loved to play tricks on the farmers and other animals. He waited until the chicken farmer brought the chickens into the coop. He unhooked the gate, ran into the coop barking and howling, and scared the feathers off the chickens. They squawked, flopping in all directions, only to fly off out of the coop and down into the pasture, where they settled on the thick, fine, green leaves of alfalfa. There they began to eat the busy green and yellow grasshoppers—which were a bother anyway. The farmer came running out of his house yelling at the coyote,

Coyote, you make me crazy, crazy, *crazy!*
Oh, Coyote, you get *out* of here, you make me so crazy!
Get away, get away!

And Coyote did just that.

Coyote went to the pig farmer's place. The pig farmer was very neat. He put the biggest pigs in the first sty, the middle-sized pigs in the middle sty, and the piglets in the third sty. The biggest pigs of all, which were the sows, were near the barn, and if one were to open *that* latch gate and bark at them, they would run, knocking down the thin fences of the other sties—and *all* the pigs would be free.

11

Coyote knew this trick.

Coyote went to the sows' latch gate. He pushed it open with his long furry yellow nose, and without a second thought, he started barking all around those big sows (who were the size of large trucks on short tires—with little corkscrew tails wiggling on their muddy rear ends). The sows ran oinking and shedding dried mud all over the dirt path to the other sties. They ran through the fences, setting every other pig free, only to race down to the open fields and upset the chickens eating grasshoppers. They ran right to the river, where they jumped into the shallow muddy water and rolled in ecstasy.

Coyote watched with sparkling eyes. The pig farmer came running out of his house waving his hat, yelling,

Coyote, you make me crazy, crazy, *crazy!*
You get *out* of here, you make me so crazy!
Get away, get away!

And Coyote did just that.

Coyote loped down to the rancher's pastures. This rancher was a very stern man. Coyote had seen him yell at his children for the *least* little mistake, and the rancher's wife never smiled—truly, she never ever smiled. At least not so Coyote could see.

Coyote never missed the rancher's cows. He ran to the big white gate, and sniffed the gate's push latch. Someone had just painted it. Coyote laughed a little to himself—oh, well, a little white paint only adds to the fun.

Coyote pushed the white bar back into the gate and shoved the gate open. Coyote's nose now was white across the top. Coyote was enjoying himself so much that this time he ran around and around the cows, stopping only long enough to show each one the white paint on his nose. The cows, who weren't too bright in the first place, were not sure what he was doing. But he was frightening them, and they began to moo, and to stamp their cloven hooves. They started to stampede the coyote, who ran down to the pasture to show the chickens his white nose.

The cows followed Coyote, scaring the chickens, who cackled loudly and woke up the pigs in the mud, who were in a moment upset by Coyote walking on them to get to the water to wash off the white paint.

The cows ended up in the river, wading in the cool clean water and curdling their milk.

Now, you know what happened next.

The rancher came running out of his house yelling and waving a pitchfork at Coyote.

Coyote, you make me crazy, *crazy, CRAZY!*
You get *out* of here, Coyote, you make me crazy!
Get away, get away!

And Coyote did just that.

Coyote hid in the bushes near the rancher's house, for he had seen the other two farmers running up to the rancher, and they were yelling something about a plan. Plans made Coyote nervous. Coyote heard the men talking. They were going to make a cage, catch Coyote, take him to

Tres Piedras, and leave him there.

Coyote did not know anything about Tres Piedras, but he did know that he had enough work *here*. The chickens needed to eat bugs if the eggs were to be large and healthy. The pigs needed some exercise, or they would fight with each other—to say nothing of getting so fat that they would be slaughtered before they had the chance to experience life fully.

The rancher needed the coyote without a doubt. If the rancher yelled and screamed at the coyote, his children could go a whole day without being yelled at, and maybe *someday* the rancher's wife would smile. It was a thought worth trying.

Coyote did not like their plan to cage and carry him.

Coyote went into town.

The town was busy with folks buying goods and sharing stories, and the children were all in school. Coyote saw the shoemaker sitting outside in the hot sun without an umbrella. The shoemaker was trying, with great difficulty, to stay awake. He had made a beautiful pair of dancing slippers, and they were just finished and ready to be put on the shelf.

Coyote knew the shoemaker would not go in and take the nap he needed unless someone would sit in the chair and sell his shoes.

Coyote nuzzled the shoemaker's arm. "Shoemaker, you are hot and tired. Please go inside and take your nap. I will watch these beautiful shoes for you."

The shoemaker scratched the coyote behind the ears. "You are a good friend—a trouble-maker, but still you are a good friend. These shoes belong to the beekeeper's daughter. They are a gift from Mr. Ramón. He is in love with the beekeeper's daughter, and he wants to take her dancing."

Coyote smiled. "Why don't I take these to the beekeeper then?"

The shoemaker shook his head. "There is this problem—Mr. Ramón wants her to have them, but he doesn't want her to know who gave them to her, for she might think him too forward. This is a problem."

Coyote smiled. "Leave it to Coyote. I will find a solution. You go now, and take your nap. If I am not here when you wake up, then you will know the problem has been taken care of. Good nap!"

The shoemaker rubbed Coyote between the shoulders and noticed his nose. The coyote's nose seemed to be more white than yellow today. Perhaps Coyote was getting old, too. The shoemaker went into this house and took a nap.

Coyote picked up the dancing slippers. They were indeed beautiful. They were made of red satin, with bright red bows sewn across the top. The heels were shiny silver, and the slippers smelled of roses.

Coyote looked around for the beekeeper. He was not in sight. Ah, yes. The beekeeper only came into town after his late lunch. Coyote ran out of town and hid in the high chokecherry bushes. He cocked his ears listening. Yes, off in the distance he heard the song.

I am the beekeeper,
I am the honey-maker,
And it's off to market I go.
I am the beekeeper,
I am the beekeeper,
I am the honey-maker,
And it's off to market I go.

Coyote smiled. He waited until the beekeeper was within barking distance, and he ran out onto the path and dropped one red slipper. Coyote quickly hid before the beekeeper could see him.

The beekeeper came upon the red slipper and stopped. He put the big dripping sack of honey down and examined the red slipper. It would fit his daughter's foot. She would like to have these slippers—but there was only one. The beekeeper looked and looked, but he could only find one slipper. "Oh, well," he said, "it was not meant to be."

He dropped the slipper back where he had found it and went on singing and walking toward town. Coyote ran quickly ahead and dropped the other slipper on the path. The beekeeper came upon this one. He put down his sack of honey and examined the red slipper.

This red slipper was exactly the same as the other. The beekeeper started to jump sideways, and then backwards, and then he scratched his head. Coyote watched, trying very hard not to laugh. The beekeeper then did something that Coyote thought was very kind. The beekeeper picked up his sack of honey and put it under the bush next to Coyote. As a matter of fact, the honey sack was leaning against Coyote's front leg!

Coyote didn't move.

The beekeeper hurried away to pick up the other slipper he had left behind on the path. Coyote smelled the honey. Coyote licked the honey sack. Coyote was very hungry. Coyote took the honey sack into the deep thick forest. He lifted the honey sack over his head and poured the honey into his mouth. He was in such a hurry that the honey dripped down the sides of his mouth onto his chest, legs, paws, back, belly, and tail. Coyote dropped the honey sack, smacking his lips.

"Ummmmm, that was delicious."

16

A fly came buzzing over to investigate the remark and landed on coyote's nose. The fly could not leave. She was stuck to his nose. Coyote tried to lift his paw to smack at the fly, but his paw was stuck to his side.

Coyote realized he was in trouble, so he began to roll on the ground—in the dirt and the leaves and the sticks—to get the drippy, sticky honey off his beautiful yellow fur. The dirt and the leaves and the sticks stuck to his sticky fur. Coyote stood up in frustration.

The fly somehow got away, but coyote was now four times his usual size, for he was carrying the forest floor stuck to him like a great, scratchy coat.

He needed to wash off in the river. The honey made him thirsty, and the sticks made him itch. Coyote limped down the river path.

The children were yelling at each other, for school was just out. Coyote called out to them for help, but when they saw him, they screamed, "Ah! A *monster*, a horrible monster, run for your lives!!"

The children disappeared, but their screams didn't. They just got louder.

Coyote was now very distressed. He prided himself on his good looks, and this was humiliating.

Coyote tried to hurry along to the river, but things poked him in places he didn't even know he had. Then Coyote heard men's voices. He pushed through the bushes to ask for help. The farmers and the rancher were there, with a cage in their hands.

When they saw Coyote, they dropped the cage and ran screaming. Coyote shook his head. The cage would never have worked. He would have figured it out in no time.

Coyote hurried on to the river and the men met him at the end of the path. They had pitchforks and shovels and long poles—and one man had a butcher knife. Coyote opened his mouth and howled when he saw that.

The men, in fear, dropped everything to run and hide behind the tall cottonwood trees.

Coyote was tired. He pulled his leafy, sticky, dirty body into the river. Oh, the water was cold, wet, and soothing, and it washed away his thirst and his excess baggage. Coyote rolled over and over and over, feeling better and better. Then Coyote looked up. On the beach were all the children, the women, and the men. They were standing there searching for the leaf monster.

Coyote paddled to shallow water. The air was cold, so Coyote stood on the sandy beach and shook his fur dry. He gave his tail an extra shake just to make sure all of the honey had washed away. The people stared at him for a while, and then, ever so slowly, the children started to laugh, and the men started to laugh, and even the rancher's wife was laughing.

The two farmers and the rancher moved forward. With tears of laughter in their eyes they said, "Coyote, we cannot take you away, for you make us laugh!"

And you know, Coyote couldn't have agreed more.

The Lizard

The blanket of soft pink clouds lifted off the mountain to unveil the bright morning sun. The father wiped his brow and smiled. He had chopped down six large trees, and with the energy he had left, he could easily chop down four more before the heat of midday.

Suddenly in front of the tree trunk stood a lizard. This lizard was as tall as a man. The lizard spoke.

"Stop this, you are killing my tree!" The lizard lifted his tongue and bared his transparent cartilage teeth. "You are a father, are you not?"

The father dropped the ax. "Yes, I have three daughters..."

The lizard interrupted him. "Then the youngest of your daughters is mine, for you almost took my life!"

The lizard spit blood and disappeared into the forest.

The father shook his head. He wiped his brow with his hand. Realizing he had come upon something most unusual, he hurried home.

His daughters ran to him when they saw him striding down the path to their small home. "Father, father, Glorieta is gone. She went to get some water from the well, and now she is gone."

The father told them of what had happened in the forest.

The lizard took Glorieta down to his big underground house. This house was surrounded by a

19

high fence with a locked gate. The lizard's house had a long hall with many heavy wooden doors. He pushed Glorieta into a small bedroom. He locked the door behind her, leaving her alone.

The lizard entered a door at the end of the hall. Here he stretched, arching his back while with his right claw he reached under his left front leg and pulled down a thread. The green lizard skin fell to the floor. A thin elderly man was revealed. He unhooked a clasp beneath his neck and lifted a mask from his head. The teeth, tongue, eyelids, shiny scalp, and lizard skin all peeled off over the old man's head.

The old man pulled on a golden-green satin robe and wrapped it around his frail body. He lay down on a big four-poster bed.

After he had rested, the man put back on his lizard skin. It was time to feed the young women. In a great kitchen, the lizard cooked up an enormous pot of mushrooms, which he ladled into a hundred bowls. The lizard put the bowls on the table in the middle of the room. The table had a hundred small silver trays on it, and each tray received a bowl. The lizard then lifted his chin and blew a sharp whistle sound through his nose. The table rose into the air. It followed the lizard out of the kitchen and into the hall.

The lizard knocked on each door in the long hall, and when it opened, he handed each young woman a bowl. When he came to Glorieta's room, she took the bowl with one hand, and with the other she pushed a wadded piece of cloth into the latch of the door. The door shut.

Glorieta waited. She listened at the door. Then she pulled on the doorknob *ever* so careful-ly. The door opened. She crept down the hall counting the doors. If she had to return, she would know which door was hers.

She tiptoed *ever* so carefully to the end of the hall. She noticed an open door, and she peered into the room.

An old man lay on the bed. He had soft grey hair. His body was very thin, and next to him on the floor lay a lizard skin.

She stepped into the doorway to look around his room. The room was full of beautiful furniture, but there were no clothes, only the lizard skin on the floor and the golden-green satin robe he wore. The man breathed out a loud sigh.

Glorieta turned and ran back the way she had come—down the hall, through the front door, out the garden, to the gate. The gate was locked. Glorieta climbed over the fence to the tunnel.

The tunnel was dark, but as she pushed herself up, heaving the dirt out of her way, she saw light. Glorieta shoved with all her might on a wooden panel. It lifted, letting her out into the forest. She ran home.

"Father, father, I am back, I escaped from the lizard's house."

Her father lifted his tired body from his blanket on the floor. He grabbed her up in his arms and held her. The two sisters got up from their blankets and began to sing and dance around them.

When breakfast was over, Glorieta told her family about her adventure.

The father shook his head. "This is not right, this is not right at all. This man is deceiving and doing harm to others. We must go down and talk to this man."

The sisters were horrified.

"No, father, leave it be. We are all here now—leave it be."

Father shook his head. "The lizard man may come back for Glorieta. He may come back for her, and take not only your youngest sister, but *all* of you. It is wrong. This is very wrong. *I will* end his deception."

The father got up from the table and put on his good hat. He reached for his ax, but his oldest daughter took it first. The father reached for his steel prying bar, but his middle daughter had it already. The father nodded, and said to his youngest daughter, "You must show us where to go."

And so they all left the house and walked together into the forest. They found the trap door and quietly went down into the lizard's world. They walked side-by-side to the lizard's gate. The middle daughter pried the gate open.

Glorieta took them to the room where she had been. After a while, there was a soft knock on the door. She opened the door cautiously, reaching out to take the bowl from the lizard's claw, and quickly closed it behind her.

Glorieta set the soup down on the table. She and her father and her sisters waited, and then quietly let themselves out, and quietly moved down the hall, opening each door they passed with the prying bar. Each room was occupied by a beautiful young woman, and each young woman was set free.

They moved on until they came to lizard's room. There on the bed lay the old man in the golden-green satin robe.

The father knelt down, crept to the lizard skin, grabbed it, and hurried back to his daughters.

They ran to the large fireplace in the great hall. They lit the fire. The damper was shut and the room soon filled with smoke. The father threw the lizard skin into the smoldering fire and watched it char and burn.

A loud wailing cry filled the air around them. "What have you done!! What have you done to my skin?"

Just as they turned to see the old man, the fireplace caved in from the heat. Even more smoke poured into the room. Glorieta and her family ran out of the house. Father carried the old man to safety.

The house crumbled.

The father said to the old man, "Sir, you have done a great wrong. Out of this wrongdoing comes your *own* lesson. One can never remain young, handsome, or strong by taking what is not rightfully his. You must learn to grow old gracefully and alone."

The father still cuts down trees for a living. Now, however, very little that happens in the forest surprises him.

The Shoes

There were two friends, two neighbors, one rich and the other poor. The poor neighbor worked for the rich neighbor, while the rich one sometimes clicked his tongue and laughed at the poor one. Finally, the poor friend decided that he should work somewhere else.

Early one morning he took all of the ashes out of his poor fireplace and loaded them into his poor broken-down wheelbarrow and pushed them to town.

The town was busy with people. They were too busy to be bothered with a poor man trying to sell ashes. The wind began to blow, and soon all the ashes were blown all over the town. The ashes even blew to the police station. The policemen came out of their dirty ashen building and fined this poor neighbor for littering. Oh, this poor, poor man! He was without money, without ashes, and now he was fined and had no way to pay.

The poor neighbor decided that he would have to sell his old wheelbarrow to get the money. A man who had some money, but not very much money, bought the wheelbarrow from the poor neighbor. The poor neighbor paid the fine and started home.

The poor neighbor was so humiliated. He would have to go home and work for his rich friend again. The poor neighbor was so sad he could hardly lift his feet. The sun beat down on his poor bare head, and burned his poor face. This poor neighbor looked down as he dragged his feet home. There on the ground was an old board. He picked it up and balanced it on his head for shade.

The sun slowly moved across the sky, and it was still hot. The poor neighbor had to walk by the river to get home. He stopped, reached into the river, and pulled out a handful of mud. He put large clumps of mud on top of his wooden hat, and put the wooden hat back on his head. Knot holes let the mud fall through all over his face, but he didn't mind, for the mud cooled him off and kept the swarming mosquitos away. He trudged on.

The poor neighbor thought about taking off his muddy wooden hat, but he was used to it by now. As he walked, he saw a fire in a clearing among the trees. He walked over to the fire and called out to the men who were there. The men saw this strange square-headed brown clumpy shape coming at them, and they ran for their lives.

The poor neighbor was saddened by this. He sat down on a log and gently pulled off his mud hat.

There next to him on the log was a large cloth bag. The poor neighbor opened the bag, for he was hungry. There in the bag were bundles of money.

The poor neighbor stumbled home in the dark with the cloth bag. He fell into his bed using the cloth bag as a pillow for his muddy head.

Early the next morning, before the sun was up, he went into town. He bought himself a new suit, some new shoes, a fancy horse with a carriage, new furniture, and some food. As he drove down the road to his poor home, he was stopped by his rich friend. "Hello, neighbor. How did you do in the big town?"

The poor neighbor smiled. "I did very well, thank you. How are you today?" Before his rich friend could answer, he drove on.

The rich friend hurried after him. "Would you like some help? I could help you unload your furniture."

The poor neighbor smiled a little more. "Sure you can help me." They spent all morning unloading the carriage and moving the furniture into the right place.

Evening came, and the rich man invited his poor neighbor over for some dinner. The poor neighbor accepted.

The rich friend had to ask. "How is it that you went into town selling ashes and you come home a rich man?"

The poor neighbor wiped his mouth as he pushed back from the table. "It wasn't ashes that made my money, it was shoes."

"Shoes? You made shoes in town?" The rich friend almost choked on his custard.

"Yes, I broke up my wheelbarrow and found some dead cow skin and made shoes. Simple shoes with simple designs. The people stood in line to buy them. Now I am out of wood and out of cowhide, so I had to retire." The poor neighbor excused himself and went home.

Early the next morning, the rich friend went to town. He took all of his money out of the bank and bought all the cowhide from the leathersmith. Then he went home to his barn and tore all the wood from the walls. The rich man loaded this into his buckboard and rode into town. He stretched the cowhide and tried to make shoes.

It rained. The leather shrank. The rich friend is not so rich anymore and the poor neighbor—well, he smiles as he rides into town.

The Magician Flea

There was a father who knew the ways of magic, and there was a boy who loved his daughter. He told the boy that if he could sleep three nights where no one could find him, the boy could marry his daughter.

The boy was a person of magic also, but the father did not know this.

The first night, the boy slept in the horns of the moon, sailing gently across the night sky. It is hard to believe, but he did. In the morning the boy came back.

"Last night you slept in the horns of the moon," said the father.

"Yes, I did," said the very surprised boy. Somehow the father had seen him sleeping in the horns of the moon.

"So where will you sleep tonight?" the father asked, smiling.

The boy did not tell him where he would sleep, for *this* time he was sure he would not be found.

That night, the boy slept inside an animal that lives in the depths of the sea. The boy was certain that the father would never find him, but that night, the father used *his* magic and found the boy sleeping inside a little animal in the depths of the sea.

When the boy arrived in the morning, the father said, "You slept in the depths of the sea."

The boy was astounded that the father knew of this. The father asked him, "God bless me, where are you going to sleep tonight?"

The boy did not answer, but thought very hard. He thought about the powers of vision this

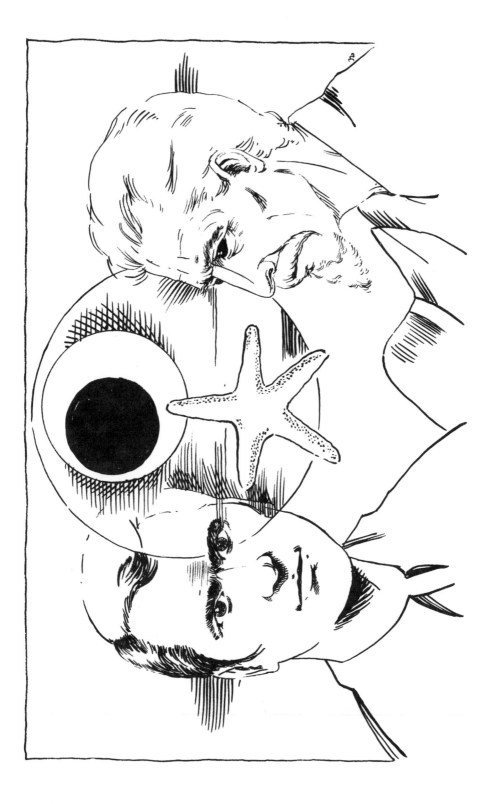

father had.

The boy left the room, stopped outside, turned himself magically into a flea, and hopped onto the door jamb. As the father walked through the door, the flea jumped on top of the father's hat. When the father went outside to do his magic, he couldn't find the boy.

The next day, when the boy came in to say "good morning" to the father, the father couldn't tell him where he had slept the night before. And the same thing happened the next day, and the same thing the day after that. The father had to give his daughter to the boy in marriage.

The boy and the daughter lived very happily, only practicing magic when they felt it was necessary—and, of course, when the father needed reminding that there is more to life than magic.

The Two Friends

There were two very old friends who didn't usually know where they were going. The story is that they went walking in front of the church. As they were passing, they saw that confessions were being heard by the priest.

One of the very old friends asked to be heard. He went into the confessional where the priest was and told his sins.

The old man then asked the priest if God was in the church.

The priest responded, "Don't you know?"

The old man questioned the priest. "Then is He lost?"

The priest answered, "Have you not found Him?"

The old man went out in a big hurry and told his friend, " Do you know, my friend, that our Father God is lost, and He hasn't finished His business with us yet."

"Then let's go home, my friend."

Witches

There was a time when the government of New Spain moved to its third capital, Santa Fe. At this time there was a fine, rich governor. He was not only fine and rich, but also perhaps handsome, clever, and humble. His name was, ah, his name was…never mind, it doesn't matter.

We had a governor. He had a fine army of soldiers. Each man was an honorable man, an honorable soldier for sure.

One of these soldiers wore his uniform proudly and was one of the most respected soldiers of Santa Fe. Yes, this young man was, he was indeed.

The young man met a woman he wanted to love, and he did. She, on the other hand, did not know he existed. This, now, is the beginning of a most tragic tale.

The soldier decided to court his young woman. Her beauty was astounding, to say nothing of her father's purse. The soldier followed the young woman everywhere she went in town. He jumped at the opportunity to open the door, and was right there with an arm to balance on when she came to steps. He even spoke to her on occasion.

The young woman ignored our soldier. How sad.

The soldier asked around town for a remedy to his problem. Someone told him of two witches who lived on the road out of town near the Church of Loretto. The soldier gathered his honor, his money, and his pride, and he marched straight to the door of the witches' house.

The door was solid wood. He pounded on it. The door opened. There stood an old woman holding a bloody spoon.

"Yes?"

"Excuse me, Madam. I am in need of your services." The soldier stood straight and tall.

"Then come in, come in, and tell us what is on your mind," the old woman replied eagerly.

The soldier entered the dark, smoky room. There was another old woman inside.

"I need a love potion."

Laughing, she asked, "A love potion, eh, dearie? Well, well, well. Let us see what we have."

A second old woman went to the cupboard and pulled out a tall thin green bottle with purple liquid in it.

"Here it is. It will cost you though, cost you a pretty penny."

The soldier responded, "I have it, I am sure. How much will it be?"

The old woman shook her head, "It's not the price in money that should trouble you—it can cost you your *love* if you're not careful."

The soldier gave them the money and took the bottle.

The next day, he met the young maiden in the square. He invited her to lunch. She accepted.

They spoke of the weather, the animals, and the village. He carefully pointed out the flowers and people around her. As she turned her head, he filled her glass with the fluid from the love potion bottle. She drank from her glass.

Nothing happened.

Another young man arrived, and smiled, and spoke, and took the young maiden home.

The soldier was furious. He threw his napkin down and paid for the lunch.

This young soldier's heart filled with anger. The love potion had cost him a lot of money, and the lunch had cost him money, and for *what?*

34

The young soldier walked down the street with the empty bottle in his hand. His training had been only in battle. The witches had tricked him to make him look like a fool. The longer he walked, the angrier he became. He strode to the witches' door.

The solid door shook with his knock. No one answered. The young soldier pounded with full force. The door slowly opened. The old woman glared at him.

"What do you want now?"

"Your love potion did not work, old woman. I want my money back!"

The woman cackled. "We said 'no guarantees', and we meant it. Go away, you foolish soldier!"

Perhaps it was the next to last word that angered him most, but we shall never know. At that moment, the young soldier did what a soldier was trained to do. He pulled out his knife and lunged at the old woman. She stepped back, he forward, and the second old woman in one motion chopped off his head.

His head rose above his body, eyes open wide, mouth round ready to call out, and then it fell to the ground and rolled. The head rolled out of the witches' doorway, and down the cobblestone street toward the square.

Every September, around the time of the Santa Fe *Fiestas*, you can hear the rolling of the head. It starts at the place they now call the oldest house on the Santa Fe Trail, and it rolls down the Santa Fe Trail to the Alameda. The witches, though, are gone and no one hears them anymore.

River Man

The man in the river has always given each of us a little of himself—a bit of humor each time we drank some of his river water. But times change and with the times come new ideas and new devices. Men came here, men with modern ways, and told us not to drink the river water because it was unclean. They were right—people had thrown garbage in the river and the water was unclean.

The men brought in clean, shiny metal pipes. The earth was dug up and channeled to hold these metal pipes that contained the water. The river and ditches no longer carried it to the people. River water was forgotten. People even forgot to throw their garbage in the river. The water slowly became clean again.

The river was not used for washing, bathing, drinking, or cooking. The great humor of the river man was untapped. We were too busy using modern appliances, piped water, and water in bottles to think of river water.

The river man was left with his humor. He was saddened that the people who had once used river water would no longer have that little smile in the morning after drinking a cup of tea or coffee made with it. He worried about the children bathing in such pure, piped water—where would their mischievousness go? And the old ones—how would they keep their crooked smiles and sparkling eyes? How would they be now?

The river man waited. He waited for a long time. He listened to the big tractors and trucks that came by. Some of them tried to change his path, but he laughed at them and went the way

38

he wished. While he waited, he worried. The river man knew that laughter and a good sense of humor keep the life alive in each of us.

The river man watched from his flowing river. He heard new babies cry—cry a *lot*. He heard small children complain and pout around their mothers and each other. The river man saw the old ones dry up in sadness. The river man didn't wait to see the old ones die. Oh, no. He made a plan.

The river man crept out of the river at night and went into people's houses. He went to the fancy new machines and pulled some wires; he went into the children's rooms and moved their toys around; he went to the old people's houses and took their false teeth.

The river man did mischief. He went to the house vaults of the rich ones, and he took their money and floated it in the river. The people became angry and irritable. We argued and fought.

One mother took her daughter out of school. She tried to teach her at home, but the little girl sat at the window and stared at the flowing river. The mother let her look, for she did not know what to do with the child.

One night, the river man came out of the river and took everyone's shadow. The children no longer had their shadows to play with. The lonely ones could no longer talk to their shadows. The old ones could no longer watch their shadows walk with them.

The little girl who lived with her mother stopped smiling, for her best friend was her shadow. She called for her shadow; she searched in the trees and the woods for her shadow. She didn't find it.

One afternoon she met a young man who was looking for his money. He was very rich, and he had seen his money mysteriously hurrying out the door toward the river early in the morning.

"Did you take my money?" the youth asked the little girl.

She laughed. "I would not take your money. I am searching for my shadow." They talked, and agreed to spend the night in a tree by the river to find out who was playing tricks. The mother gave her daughter some extra food for the young man.

The youth fell asleep, but not the little girl. She watched. She saw a man with long flowing silver hair come running from the town to the river. He ran right into the river and disappeared. She woke the young man, who just caught a glimpse of the old man's hair floating down into the river. The young man was greedy, and he wanted his money back. He dived into the river to get the old man. The girl dived in after him, for she feared what he would do to the old man.

Down they swam to an underwater house. They peered through the window. There were black shapes in the house, and the little girl recognized her shadow. She pushed open the door, and the young man followed her. The door slammed behind them. There stood the old man with the long flowing silver hair.

"What are you doing in my house?" the river man asked with a big grin.

"We are looking for things that we lost. Who are you?"

"I am the river man. I am the one who brings humor and joy into the lives of those that use my river water."

They listened to him. His wonderful, warm face glowed with a grand smile. They were happy to have found him and almost forgot all about their things. When at last the river man said he was tired, for he had had a busy night, they took what they needed. The young man only took a little of his money, and the girl took her shadow.

"If those who have things here will come to the river and use the river water, they will get their things back." The old man smiled and nodded off to sleep.

The next morning, the young man and the little girl went into town and told their story of the river man and his mischief and of the river water. The people were angry. How dared this river man make so much trouble for them! They went to the river, and those who tried to swim in it were amazed at how happy they felt. Those who washed their faces in the clean river water felt their lips stretch across their faces in almost-forgotten smiles. Slowly, small items came floating up from the river. The people—all of us—laughed and played in the water.

The river water brought joy, friendship, generosity, and good will back to us. The river man did not come up, but the flowing water rippled and slapped against the riverbank. We knew that he was pleased.

We use the river water every day now for different things, as we used to do, but now we use it and it brings balance to our lives. We respect the river and keep it clean.

In the reflection of the river water, we can see our own smiles. Look, and you can see yours, too.

Chicken Dinner

The day was warm and wet. The evening before had brought heavy rain storms and many travelers. A farmer stood in his field studying the clouds when a traveler happened to walk over to him.

"Yes, it will rain again tonight, I am sure of it," the traveler said.

The farmer smiled. "Well, that is your opinion. The clouds are thinning to the east. The rain is moving northwest. Perhaps we will have some dry weather, and I can get my hay baled."

The traveler nodded. "Perhaps, yes. You know, I believe you are right."

The farmer invited this young man to dinner. "We have two travelers who are already inside, but come, let us eat."

The traveler followed the farmer into the kitchen. The farmer's wife was pulling up the extra chairs. The farmer patted the young man on the shoulder. "Since you are our last guest, you may serve the meal."

The young man studied the platter of food. What a meal it was! The chicken was baked a golden brown, the rich lemon gravy sauce was thick with onions and mushrooms, the potatoes were beaten into creamy mounds, and the bowls of fresh vegetables glistened with butter.

The young man sat down in his high-backed chair, took up the carving knife, and began with the chicken.

"The head of this magnificent bird should go to the man of this fine establishment…"

The young man placed the head of the chicken on the farmer's plate.

"The neck of such a fine animal should go to the woman who respectfully cares for her farmer…"

The neck of the chicken was placed on the farmer's wife's plate.

"Ah, this lovely daughter will soon be ready to fly away. Her face and her lovely manner show the beauty of her age. *She* shall receive the wing…"

The wing of the chicken was placed on the farmer's daughter's plate.

"This strong young man certainly is ready to start his own farm. Soon he, too, will fly—to his own land, rich in soil. Therefore he shall *also* receive a wing…"

The farmer's son's plate now held a chicken wing.

"The traveler to my left is rubbing his leg, and a leg he shall have to help him on his journey…"

A leg was put upon the older traveler's plate.

"This fellow on my right—he, too, has walked far and has much farther yet to go. So, he also shall have a leg…"

The other leg was given to the other traveler.

"Thanks be to God. That leaves what little is left for me…"

And he gracefully laid the rest of the plump juicy chicken on his very own plate.

43

The Mare

Every day a farmer walked his land. It held hard dirt, a dirt that needed much plowing. He did not like to plow by himself, for it was difficult to pull the plow and to guide the plow at the same time. As a matter of fact, it was impossible.

There were times when his dear wife would try to help him, but she was expecting their fourth child, and the other children were still small and got into all sorts of trouble if left alone for even a moment.

The farmer knew he must find a solution to his problem. He walked toward town. On the road, he noticed the monastery. It had thick, rounded adobe walls that held strength, peace, and religion. He smiled, for the thought of becoming a monk had often crossed his mind. Then, out of the corner of his eye he spotted an animal. There near the monastery stood a strong mare, penned in a small corral. Her eyes were glazed with boredom. This gave the farmer an idea.

The farmer knocked on the monastery door. The noise echoed through the quiet air. At last, the heavy carved wooden door opened, revealing a man with a solemn face, dressed in a hooded brown robe.

"Bless you, my son," the voice whispered through the stillness.

The farmer hesitated and then spoke firmly. "Bless you, also. May I inquire about the mare in the corral next to the monastery? Is she for sale? "

The monk shook hid head. "She is the horse of the monastery. She is one of us."

The farmer continued, "Sir, I am in desperate need of a horse to help me on my farm. I live but ten miles from here, and if I could borrow her, have her stay at my stable, and care for her and work her and treat her well, I could return her every Sunday for prayers."

There was silence. Then, "Wait here."

The monks decided after a time that the farmer could take the mare, although she was to be in her stable at the monastery by dawn on Sunday. She could be taken again on Monday morning.

The farmer went to the stable. He walked around the mare, patting her, talking to her, the way one should when he is taking someone away from her home. The farmer led the mare to the gate, opened the gate, sat on the mare, and gave her a good gentle kick. She did not move.

"Hey, giddy-up."

The mare did not move.

"Yoo-hah!" the farmer called out.

The mare turned and glared at him. The farmer got off. He knocked on the monastery door. The door opened. "Bless you, my son."

"Bless you, also. How does the mare move?"

"Bless you, again, my son. You say 'Thanks be to God,' and she will move."

The farmer went out to the mare. He sat firmly on her back and said firmly, "Thanks be to God!" The mare took off at a dead run.

The farmer felt the strength of the horse. They raced to his home. The farmer's dear wife stood outside waving at him.

"Dinner is ready!" she called. "What a fine horse."

The last words were muted in the farmer's ears, for the horse did not stop. She ran the length of the land, only to return to the stable at the monastery.

There was once again a knock at the monastery door.

"Bless you, my son."

"Bless you, also. How do you get the mare to stop?"

"Bless you, again, my son. You say 'Hail Mary full of grace.'"

The farmer rubbed the mare down, gave her some oats, and once more took her to the open gate.

"Thanks be to God."

The mare raced out of the gate straight for his home. He pulled the mare's mane to the right, heading her toward his stable, and called out, "Hail Mary full of grace!"

The mare stopped in her tracks. The farmer led her into his stable and bedded her down for the night.

The work was so much easier with the mare.

One afternoon as the farmer was riding home from the fields, a lightning storm came upon the land. The lightning came down two inches from the mare's rump.

The mare took off, racing across the mesa in a frenzied fear.

The edge of the mesa was nearing fast, and the mare and the farmer would plummet to their deaths. The farmer was so frightened that he could not recall the words he needed to stop the mare.

The farmer lifted his face heavenward, and called out, "Hail, Mary, full of grace, the Lord be with me."

The mare, upon hearing the words, came to a dead stop not a hoof's width from the edge of the cliff. She was not even two *hairs* away from death. The farmer wiped his brow, and said, "Thanks be to God."

47

Owl Wishes

I sit watching my woman sleep. The baby boy nestled in the curve of her arm is only minutes old. I listen to his breathing. It is not an easy sound. It is the sound of struggle.

I helped deliver this baby, our baby. His birth was difficult. The difficulty now is with my wife. She has gone to sleep, and I cannot wake her.

Her breathing stops. I pray for it to return.

An owl in the barn hoots. The hoots are loud, startling sounds. My wife breathes.

I stand up to look out the window. Where is the owl? By the grain room in the barn? Lights glow in the dark night. There are lights in the loft. I run to the barn and up the stairs two at a time, for I do not want to be gone long from my wife.

Burning red eyes of coal stare at me. A *bruja*, a witch, cackles. "You love your wife more than the boy?"

Her eyes make me tremble, but I answer honestly, "Yes, she is my wife."

The witch hoots, her long curved fingers pointing at me. "Why?"

I must be honest, for to lie to a witch means death. "My wife is the woman who carries my love. Without her, I must carry my own love. Life would be a burden."

The witch's eyes glow. "The boy loves you."

"No, *he* is just beginning to live. My wife is just beginning to love life."

The witch turns away. "Go. Your wife lives, for you are honest in your heart."

I run back to the house and through the hall to the bedroom. My wife is sitting up, smiling. My boy nurses at her breast. The barn is dark; the owl has gone.

I lie down next to my wife, and we sleep.

48

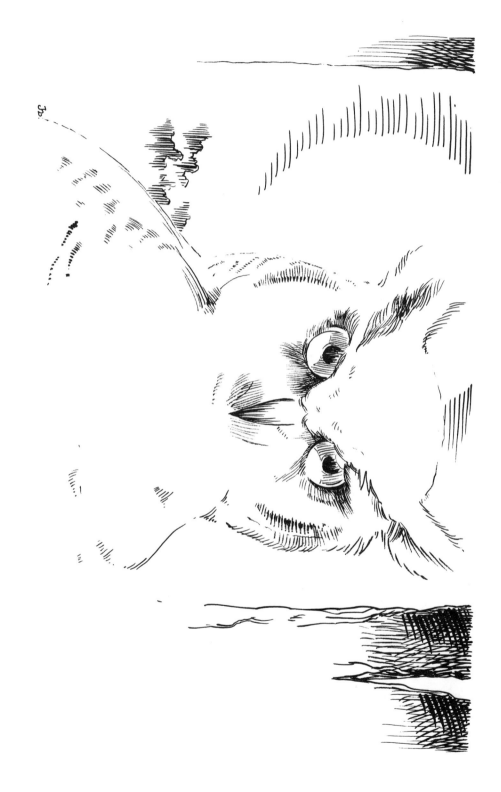

Leticia's Turtle

Every day an old beggar woman came to Leticia's home. Leticia shared her food with the beggar woman although Leticia barely had enough food for her own family.

At the market on one particular morning, Leticia saw a fine plump chicken for sale. She took all her money, bought the plump chicken, and hurried home to put it in the boiling pot. Her husband and children would be pleased with dinner tonight.

Leticia was cleaning the house when she heard a knock at the door. She closed her eyes and prayed, "Please, please, not the beggar woman. Not tonight."

She went to the door, and there was the beggar woman.

Leticia let her in, carefully guiding her away from the kitchen. They talked while Leticia cleaned. The sun was sinking in the sky. Leticia grew angry thinking that the woman would insist on staying for dinner and eat up the plump chicken.

Finally, Leticia said, "Thank you for stopping by, but now you must be going."

The beggar woman's face turned white. She had never been turned out without supper before. She would go hungry tonight. The beggar woman said good night and left.

Leticia hurried to the kitchen. Flies flew in through the windows in droves. They buzzed all around the pot of chicken. Leticia tried to shoo them away, but they came back. They buzzed around her head. They crawled all over her pretty tablecloth and plates.

Leticia's husband came home. The children finished with their chores and came in. They sat down at the table, shooing away the flies.

50

"I am very hungry tonight," said the husband. "What is for dinner?"

Leticia smiled. "Something very special. Wait and see."

"Our beggar woman isn't here," the children whispered. "Maybe we should wait for her."

Leticia heard them. "Hush children, here is your dinner."

Leticia lifted up the big pot of chicken and began to pour it into the serving bowl. Instead of chicken, a *turtle* fell out!

The turtle climbed out of the serving bowl onto the table, and from the table to the floor, where it hurried out the door.

The husband yelled to the oldest child, "Run, run get the priest. We have been bewitched."

The child ran away, and returned with the priest. The priest nodded when he heard the story. "You have shared when you had only a little food. Now, when you have plenty, you will not share. It was a curse of God. You must remember to respect others."

From that day on, they invited the beggar woman to have dinner with them, and in return, she told them wonderful stories.

Wise Stones

A father had three daughters who were very beautiful, very strong, and very clever. When the father fell ill, he got up from his bed and prayed before *la Virgen de Guadalupe.*

"What my daughters desire of life," he asked, "please give them. They are deserving of what they wish."

The father died.

The land was divided among the three daughters. The youngest thanked God for her gift. The middle one thanked God for her gift. The oldest said, "How awful! Now I must work my land alone, and I am not a slave!"

She was filled with anger.

One day, a stranger walked across their lands. She carried herself in the manner of a wise woman. She asked the youngest daughter why she was clearing the field.

"I am clearing my field so that I can grow chilis to share with my sisters and to sell to my neighbors."

The wise woman walked to the second daughter. "What are you clearing your fields for?"

The second daughter replied, "Alfalfa for my horses and my sisters' horses—and also to sell in town, for I will grow the best alfalfa in all the valley."

The wise woman walked to the oldest daughter. "My daughter, why are you clearing your fields?"

This was not a good time to ask the oldest daughter, for she was angry. She had come across a whole part of the field that was packed with stones. She had hurt her back pulling them up, only to find more and more. "I am growing stones," she replied angrily. "They come up one after another." The oldest daughter bent again over her work.

The fall came, and the sisters went out to harvest their crops.

The youngest sister had big, fat, ripe red chilis. They were better than any she had ever tasted.

The second sister harvested fields of green, thick-leaved alfalfa, lush and rich.

The third sister sat in her field in tears of sadness. Her field was filled with stones. The more she tried to clear the stones, the more would appear. Her two sisters came up and comforted her. They could not understand her hardship.

Meadowlark

A young boy raced out of the house early in the morning. He ran down the path to the forest. There he sat, still and listening. Wings rustled nearby, and then the meadowlark sang.

Every day the song would pierce the air, lifting the animals of the forest out of their hiding places. They would all listen. The boy felt honored and special, for it was as if each morning the meadowlark waited for him to arrive before she sang.

The boy ran home. He raced into his mother's kitchen, grabbing at her skirt and calling out, "Mother, mother, you should have heard the meadowlark today. Oh, mother, it sang so beautifully and it waited, it waited for me. Oh, mother, come hear the song of the meadowlark."

The mother stood watching her son. She pulled her skirt out of his hands. "You who listen to birds, go, get out of here. Go down to the field and help your father with the work. Go!"

The boy then raced to his father. "Father, father, you should have been there! The meadowlark sang, again she sang, and the song this morning was more beautiful than the last. Oh, father, come with me to the forest, and let's listen to the meadowlark."

The father shook his head, but with a smile he said, "You come here and take this shovel. We have much work to do."

The two of them worked. The boy talked on and on about the meadowlark, and the father thought his own thoughts.

Men from other places were moving onto the adjoining lands and taking over his water from the ditch. They were putting up fences and bringing in cattle that knocked down the fences and ate his crops.

The winter was poor. They hardly had any food. He watched their life grow poor.

One morning, the boy got up early and raced out to the forest. The meadowlark sang her song of joy. The boy sat and thought of how he could get the bird to sing to his parents. This bird could bring them some happiness. He came up with an idea.

He could trap the meadowlark and bring her home. He could feed her, and she would sing, bringing joy to the hearts of his hard-working parents.

The first day, the boy made a cage.

The second day, he took it to the forest and placed it in a tree.

The third day, he put food in the cage and waited.

The fourth day, he trapped the meadowlark.

He carried her home. He showed her to his mother who was busy. She put the cage up high, hanging from a wooden beam in the ceiling.

Every morning the boy ran to the forest and gathered berries and bugs to feed the meadowlark.

The meadowlark sang and sang.

The brutal cold winds that sting the soul blew from the north. The food was gone. Mother was up every day trying to fix something that would keep them alive. Father stoked the fire, hoping the wood would hold, and knowing it wouldn't. The boy went to the forest to gather what food he could find to feed the meadowlark.

The meadowlark sang, and whether they knew it or not, the song kept the family fed in spirit.

One morning as the boy raced for the door, his father scooped him up in his arms. "Where are you going in such a hurry every morning?"

The boy wriggled for his freedom. "I go to the forest to get food for the meadowlark."

The father dropped the boy on his feet. "What? You race through the cold snow, letting the heat out of the house, to gather food for the bird?"

"The bird sings beautiful songs," said the boy.

The father reached up to the cage. He opened the cage and pulled out the meadowlark. He took the meadowlark in his strong hands, and with one swift gesture, he broke her neck. The bird dropped from his hands to the clean dirt floor.

The boy stared at the dead bird in disbelief. Then, all at once, the father's eyes rolled back, his face went white, his hands started to shake, and the father fell to the floor, dead, next to the beautiful meadowlark.

Mother walked into the room. She gasped, and reached for her son. "What…what has happened?"

The boy turned to her. "Mother, my mother, we can live without food for a time, we can live without heat for a time, but we cannot live without the spirit of song."

The Wooden Horse

Pablo helped Grandfather cut the soft pine wood into rectangles. Some of the wooden rectangles were very small—as small as your smallest finger. The smaller pieces were cut by Grandfather, carefully, with a hand ax. The larger wooden squares were cut by Pablo with a long ax. Pablo and his grandfather lived high on a hill that looked out over the village.

Grandfather sat down on an old tree trunk. "Pablo, I cannot carry all of this today. Would you take the cut wood to our roadside stand, cover it, and come back to eat? Then we can go back down to the road with our arms free."

Pablo agreed. Grandfather was ninety years old; his ripeness of age had taken his youthful energy. Pablo was fourteen years old, and was taller and stronger than Grandfather this summer. Pablo wrapped the cut wood in a burlap sack. He went down the path to the roadside stand.

Some of Grandfather's carving tools were already there. His sign banged back and forth in the morning breeze. It read "Benjamin Ortega, woodcarver."

Grandfather carved beautiful little animals, such as birds, beavers, squirrels, and cats. These small animals he pegged to branches of wood which were pegged into a tall round base that looked like a tree. Tourists would come and buy Grandfather's carvings.

Pablo thought Grandfather wouldn't mind his being a little late. He jumped the low wooden fence that ran along the ditch and hurried to a path that led to an old gray barn.

There were some other boys there. They were clicking their tongues trying to get señor

Ortiz's new colt to gallop in the field. Pablo did not go to them.

He turned to look at the black stallion the Ortizes were selling. The horse was called *Relámpago*—which means "lightning."

Pablo wanted that horse, for he was sure he could win any rodeo prize or go anywhere in the world on Relámpago.

Grandfather had said no. They could barely afford to live themselves, never mind to own a fine, fat, well-bred stallion such as Relámpago.

Relámpago stamped his feet in the stall. His mighty black head swung back and forth, desperate for the freedom to gallop. Pablo wanted to run to the gate, climb on the sleek black back, and ride off into a better world.

Instead, Pablo ran home. He heard Grandfather in the kitchen cooking breakfast. Pablo went to his little cot in the corner of the room and pulled out a bundle of cloth. He carefully unwrapped it. There in his hand he held a large oval shape of pine. The wood was smooth and dark from years of work. Pablo gently stroked it.

His father had started to carve a horse out of this oval of pine when Pablo was just a baby. His father had been killed in the Vietnam war. His mother had saved the barely-begun horse, and sometimes when Pablo was frightened, she let Pablo sleep with it—that is, she did until she died from pneumonia.

Pablo rubbed the wood with his fingers. He could finish this piece. His carving was good, for he had learned a great deal from watching his grandfather.

Grandfather did not know about the horse. Pablo decided that today he would work on it. Someday it would be finished. Someday very soon he would sell it for a real horse.

Pablo wrapped the wooden horse in its cloth and hid it in his shirt. Grandfather called to

59

him, "Pablo, where are you? Breakfast is ready." Pablo hurried to the kitchen to eat.

Once the dishes were washed and the food stored and Grandfather had finished with his morning duties, they went on their way to the roadside stand. Pablo let Grandfather lean on him as they walked down the steep hill to the road.

People were waiting when they arrived at the stand.

Pablo watched as Grandfather talked with the people.

Grandfather was busy, and Pablo was preoccupied with the thought of the black stallion.

The bundle in his shirt was ready for carving. Pablo sat down under a tree behind the roadside stand. Grandfather was so busy that he would not notice his grandson's work behind him.

Pablo pulled his bundle out of his shirt and began to whittle on it. Every now and then people would come around him and watch. Pablo kept working. He steadied his hand and worked on the arch over the horse's eye, and then on the careful shape of each eye. The sweat from Pablo's brow dripped down his cheek. He lifted his head to watch Grandfather.

Grandfather was too busy to notice Pablo, and so Pablo continued. He worked until the sun was on the horizon and it was time to help Grandfather close the roadside stand.

They packed up their work and started for home. Grandfather did not cross the road right away, but walked along the ditch path by the low wooden fence.

They heard a truck's motor roar nearby. Pablo saw a large horse trailer pull away from the Ortiz's barn. It drove by the boy and his grandfather and turned onto the main highway. Relámpago was stamping his hooves and snorting in the back of the big silver horse trailer as it drove out of sight.

Pablo gasped when he saw this. His lip quivered as the horse was driven away. Pablo quickly looked down, for he didn't want his grandfather to know of his feelings.

Grandfather said nothing, and kept walking home. They laid down the carving tools, the cut wood, and the money box. Grandfather put his hand on Pablo's shoulder, and with his other hand he pulled the bundle out from Pablo's shirt.

"Pablo, you have one of the finest horses in all of Chimayo right here."

Pablo smiled. He would carve more horses, perhaps even one as fine as Relámpago.

The River

"Papá, the sky, it is grey again."

"Don't worry, my daughter, it is good."

"Papá, the river, it is rising higher every minute."

"Yes, my daughter, it is life. It is the sweet water of the old ones and of the souls. It is good."

His gnarled fingers thrust the shovel deeper into the dirt. The wind thrashed my long blue cotton skirt around my legs.

The river had been miles away, yet I could see it now. As father would say, the river was "swollen with life." The shovels around us worked at the same rhythm as my father's.

Papá, dear Papá, his brown eyes calm, filled with love for the natural way of things. Papá accepts what will be and what will come. The men understood Papá.

They trusted Papá.

The river didn't know him, it just kept rising. The water surged, rippled, tore the earth apart.

Papá kept the shovel moving in and out, turning, pushing the earth. The dry dirt we had been standing on was now mud. Papá kept shoveling.

I moved to stand beside my oldest. She was fourteen; she was shoveling. She looks a lot like my mother. My mother was here somewhere—I knew it. I could feel her presence. Perhaps Papá could, too.

I looked up at him. His eyes were sad. Sweat poured down from his brow, and his teeth gripped his lower lip as he shoveled.

The pain of losing my mother was always there inside him, yet he would not talk about it. The fear of the flood woke him at night when the ditch frogs stopped croaking. The pain was strong, still there.

My mother died in a flood, a flood that washed through the land unexpectedly. Papá never said anything about it. He accepted the ways of this earth, and respected life and death.

My oldest daughter shoveled as her Grandpapá did. She lifted the earth and pushed the rich wet soil the same as Papá did. My Papá was, in her eyes, her father, too.

My husband could not live here with us. He had worked the land, the land had worked him, and the land had won. I lost my husband; my children lost their father. He lives in California now, and we live here on the land.

Papá put his shovel down, and he nodded with his chin to the house he had built for his woman, my mother. The seepage of the river water was weakening the walls. The front wall of the kitchen was sinking. The adobe mud wall was slithering down to the earth, where it had been born.

I grabbed my youngest, throwing her over my hip. We ran for the house and gathered up what we could in wheelbarrows and red wagons. We pushed my father's belongings to higher ground.

I went back to the digging. Papá nodded at me. His eyes were sad, his arms tired. He pointed to the house. "That was your mother's kitchen, your mother's home. The river is taking from me again."

63

I shoveled beside him. My shovel was working faster than his. The other men began to leave, talking about their homes, their families, and the river. Still it rose, sloshing against our boots, defeating our work.

Some markers floated past us. The markers were set in the bank of the river to show how high the water would rise each year. The river was bringing its own markers.

Papá picked one of the markers from the water. "This marker is for me. I have worked this land, built on this land, helped your mother give birth to all of you on this land—and the river…the river takes it all back." He wiped his brow, tossed his hat on his head, and said, "I am going to the river to check the markers."

He threw his shovel to me, hard, and walked away.

I stood for some moments before I realized what Papá had said. Papá had always told us to leave the markers, that the markers should be left alone.

"Papá, Papá, wait. Papá, wait!"

There was no answer. There was just the river, rolling in force.

Papá had said, "Water is life, the life it takes from us is its life to give again."

I called out, "Papá, Papá."

All I heard was the wind.

"Go with love, Papá. Go with God."

The Flea

Once there was and was not a rich landowner. He loved to laugh; he loved a good joke as well as any fellow. Best of all, he loved to make riddles that no one could answer. One day the rich landowner came back from a long ride across his land. He was hot and tired but in a good mood. As his worker helped him remove his heavy riding jacket, a flea jumped from the jacket to the rich landowner's nose. The rich landowner put up his hands for all to be quiet, and with one swift gesture he caught the flea in his hand.

He smiled gleefully, for now he had a great idea. He told his worker to run quickly for the *mayordomo*, the landowner's steward, and to tell him it was urgent he see him right away. The worker ran, returning with the *mayordomo* who was anxious to know what was so important that he had to be taken away from his work.

The landowner took the *mayordomo* into his study and talked with him privately. The rich landowner asked the *mayordomo* to put out his hand. The rich landowner put the tiny flea in the *mayordomo*'s hand.

"Don't crush it. I want you to feed this flea until it is the size of a cow. Don't tell anyone what it is. You yourself will lose your life if anyone finds out what I have asked of you. Now go, and come back to me when that flea is the size of a cow." The *mayordomo* nodded that he understood and left the rich landowner chuckling to himself.

You can be sure that the *mayordomo* did not tell anyone at all about the flea. First of all, he didn't want anyone to know of such a crazy idea, and second, he did not want to lose his life.

He was a married man with seven children, and his job paid well. *Sí, como no.*

Well, the rich landowner's wife gave birth to their first child, a beautiful girl. Shortly after her birth, the landowner's wife became very ill and died, leaving the landowner with the responsibility of raising the daughter himself. She grew quickly and well, and she loved to laugh as much as her father. Soon she was ten, and then her fourteenth birthday arrived and along with it many young men who wanted to court her. Her father became very strict and sent the young men away from the house.

One day the *mayordomo* came to the rich landowner. The rich landowner asked, "What brings you here, my good man?" The *mayordomo* reminded the landowner of the flea.

The landowner laughed and laughed. "Oh, yes, now and then I would think of that flea. Is it as big as a cow?"

The *mayordomo* shook his head. "Well," he said, "the flea is as big as a small calf. However, sir, the flea is now very old, and I fear that soon it might die."

The landowner told the *mayordomo* to wait until dark and bring the flea to the barn. There should be no one else, or else.

That night the rich landowner and the *mayordomo* sat in front of the flea. The flea could hardly breathe, it was so fat and so old. The landowner patted the flea and said, "Good-bye, flea. Your life will not be forgotten or wasted. You will still be put to good use."

The flea died, and the rich landowner and the *mayordomo* skinned it. The *mayordomo* saddled up the landowner's best horse, and the landowner rode out into the night. He rode to a small town far to the north, to the home of an Indian drum maker. The old Indian welcomed the landowner, for wealth always followed the landowner. The landowner talked late into the night with the drum maker. Then the landowner rode home.

67

Three weeks passed, and the landowner saddled his horse late in the night and rode back to the old Indian drum maker. The landowner picked up a perfectly round tambourine, which he kept until his daughter's sixteenth birthday. On that day he gave it to her, telling her it would be the riddle that must be answered if she were to be married.

The daughter invited all her friends to a party, and she danced with her new tambourine. When she finished, her father clapped his hands.

"Whoever can tell me what this tambourine is made of may marry my daughter." The landowner's eyes sparkled with glee.

Many of the young men ran to him and, kneeling, told him that it was made from a goat skin, or a calf skin, or a sheepskin. The landowner laughed and laughed. They were all wrong. The daughter thought this was a good test, for she loved her father and hated the thought of having to leave him if she married.

The riddle lasted a long time—well into the daughter's seventeenth year. The landowner was by now tired of this riddle and of the thoughtlessness of the young men who tried to answer. He decided that anyone who did not answer the question correctly should be horse-whipped. That way they could have some privacy and not be so bothered by suitors. It worked. Very few men came to try the riddle.

Now, up in the hills above Chimayo there happened to be a sheepherder and his family. The youngest of the boys heard of this riddle. He thought that if he answered the question he would have money and a beautiful wife. He had always had to wear his brothers' clothes, eat last, and be the first one blamed if the sheep were lost.

He decided that since he was fourteen, he would like to try his best for the rich landowner's daughter. He said good-bye to his family and put half a tortilla in his pocket. His mother

68

wept at the thought of her little boy getting a whipping.

There is something you should know about this young sheepherder. He had spent most of his life walking up and down mountains, so he had a difficult time walking on the flat path to the rich landowner's home. As the boy walked along, he kept tripping and falling flat. At one point he fell right down on an ant hill. He lifted his head, and there before him was a large red ant with its stinger straight out, ready to sting him.

The sheepherder said, "Oh, please don't hurt me. I fell by accident. I mean you no harm."

The ant said, "All right, but for the inconvenience of landing on my ant pile, I would like to ask you to carry me to town, for I would like to see what goes on there."

The sheepherder thought for a moment and said, "Well, I am going to the rich landowner's home first, but then I could take you to the town. Here, get in my pocket."

So they started off, and the ant wondered at the sheepherder, for he had not taken a bath in many, many months and the smell was quite strong.

Soon the sheepherder forgot that the land was flat and tripped over his own feet. This time when he fell, he almost hit a tree. On the tree was a fine fat beetle sunning himself. The beetle was frightened at this body coming at him and turned, ready to hide. The sheepherder lifted himself on one elbow and apologized for scaring the beetle.

The beetle asked where he was going, and the sheepherder told him. The beetle asked, "Can I go with you? I would like to see the inside of the rich landowner's home." And so the beetle joined the ant in the sheepherder's pocket. The beetle expressed alarm at the smell of the sheepherder, but then sheepherders are known for not taking baths.

The sheepherder had gone quite a ways when there was a bridge. The boy was so interested in the sides of the bridge that he forgot once again about his feet, and he fell. This time he fell inches away from a field mouse. The field mouse was a brave mouse and ran up to the sheepherder to lecture him about being more careful.

The sheepherder apologized and offered the mouse some of his tortilla in apology. Once the mouse heard of the journey, he wanted to come too. And so the ant, the beetle, and the field mouse shared the half tortilla with the sheepherder. Then they climbed into his pocket.

Before the afternoon sun could give long shadows to the tall trees, they came to the landowner's house. The sheepherder called out to the gatekeeper. The gatekeeper let him in, though he was shaking his head, for this boy was so young it would be a shame if he got a whipping.

The housekeeper opened the door for the shepherd boy. She had tears in her eyes. I am not sure if they were from sympathy or because the boy smelled so strongly.

The rich landowner left his bookkeeper and met the young boy. "Are you sure that you want to do this? You will be whipped if you guess wrong, you know that, don't you?"

The boy nodded.

The daughter came into the room dancing with the tambourine. She danced round and round, careful not to get too close, for the boy smelled disgusting. When she finished, the rich landowner asked the boy if he knew what the skin of the tambourine was—and would he *please* hurry, for the air in the room was thickening.

The boy asked if he could hold the tambourine. As he moved forward to take it from the daughter, he tripped over his feet and fell. The ant was thrown out of his pocket onto his sleeve. The boy got up and took the tambourine. The daughter was so disgusted by this boy that she was ready to cry. The ant crawled down the boy's sleeve onto the tambourine and

70

walked across it. Then the ant crawled back up the sleeve to the collar of the jacket and called to the sheepherder.

"This tambourine is made from a flea's skin. I know flea skin, for one winter I shared my food with one."

The sheepherder studied the tambourine. It looked to him more like sheepskin.

Then the beetle, who wanted to know what was going on, crawled out onto the tambourine. He was climbing the boy's sleeve when the boy started toward the daughter to return the tambourine. As he did so, you can guess, he fell again. With that, the beetle landed up in his hair. The beetle edged down and hid behind the boy's ear.

The rich landowner called to the boy. "What is this tambourine made of, my son?"

The beetle tickled the sheepherder's ear and said, "It is a flea skin. Tell him it is a flea skin. Fleas are my cousins and this is a flea skin."

The sheepherder nodded his head saying, "All right, all right. It is a flea skin. I got it—it is a *flea skin!*" The sheepherder said it twice so that the beetle would stop tickling his ear.

The rich landowner stood up aghast. The daughter threw herself at her father's feet. "Please, please, father, don't make me marry this boy. He is awful. He stinks!"

The sheepherder put out his hand. "Wait a minute. It is up to *me* if I want to marry you or not. Is that not right?"

The father said, "Yes, that is right. Daughter, I am a man of my word. It is up to this boy." The sheepherder was going to walk over to them, but decided against it. The beetle whispered in the boy's ear. "Don't take this woman. She is spoiled by too many rich things. Besides, she is too old for you. Ask for gold instead."

The boy thought this over and repeated what the beetle advised him. The father and daughter were most relieved. The rich landowner asked the sheepherder how much money he would like to have. The sheepherder pulled his pouch from his pocket. He had always dreamed of having his little pouch filled with money. "I would like money up to the top of my pouch as I stand here holding it."

The landowner called his bookkeeper and told him to bring gold.

The mouse had now awakened because there was no more falling or swaying, and he stuck his head out of the pocket to see what was happening. He heard the last of the sheepherder's request and thought this boy needed his help. The mouse climbed down the sleeve of the sheepherder's jacket and into the pouch. As the mouse ate a hole in the bottom of the pouch. As the bookkeeper returned to fill it, the money fell on the boy's feet. The boy did not move, though, for the mouse was now on his shoulder telling him to hold his hands still and not say a word.

The rich landowner was as good as his word. He let the money fall through the hole in the pouch and soon the mountain of money was up as high as the top of the pouch which the patient sheepherder held.

The landowner asked if there was one more request that the sheepherder wanted to ask. The sheepherder listened to the mouse and repeated what he heard. "Yes, I need a nice wagon and two good horses to help me pull this money back to Chimayo."

The landowner was only too happy to have the sheepherder leave.

The sheepherder waved and went on his way. The ant decided that he had had enough excitement and wanted to go home. The beetle was dropped off at the landowner's barn to visit some friends, and the mouse, well, he wanted to go back to Chimayo with the sheepherder.

The young sheepherder married when he was sixteen. He married a girl he had known since he was little, and they lived in a nice modest house and had many children.

Remember

The people came in the daytime. They tried to speak with his parents, but his parents didn't understand them. The people brought him to this place from the Indian Reservation when he was very small. They brought him to the boarding school in the winter.

They brought him to the nuns, and the nuns loved him. He was pure, clean, untouched.

They taught him after hours; they fed him sweets; they spoiled him.

He was beautiful. He was like a book, a small psalm book with pages of fine thin tissue, edges dipped in gold leaf. He was fragile, kind, unsure.

A man and a woman adopted him. They brought him here to the city, and they loved him.

They took him to church; they gave him clothes; they taught him how to eat. They even gave him a name of their own choosing.

They did not know that he was still his own person. He was not a part of them—he was himself.

He grew tall, strong, brave. They showed him how to think as they thought. They showed him how to dress as the best men dressed. He was quiet, polite, diligent. He was sent off again to boarding school until he was sixteen.

When he graduated, the boarding school sent him home to his adopted parents. They sent him to the place where they believed he belonged, but they did not know him. He listened to the songs of the women. He learned of the money-making schemes. He rode the horses, and with time he grew wise. He was thoughtful, careful, cautious.

73

He stayed with them until he was twenty. He met a woman, a strong woman with fine breasts, good spirit, a will to live. He wished for her, longed for her, dreamed of her.

His adopted parents spoke to him of the other women in the city—the women with money, houses, power. He listened, but he knew what he wanted. He would get his woman, the one he desired, for he knew the ways of these people. He planned, schemed, arranged. He married her in the spring with the other wedding parties.

She was strong. She loved him firmly. She gave herself to him with dedication. He was proud. She wanted to live with her people. He wanted to please her. So they packed, cleaned, moved. He helped her with the new home. He worked, struggled, gave to her what she needed. She wanted him to speak the language of her people. He studied, listened, followed her.

He woke up and saw her beauty. The long woven dresses, the flowering beauty, the rhythm of the dances awakened his soul. He was home with these people, and at last he was content. He knew the ways of this place, for he remembered.

We do not know him, now.

He knows himself.

74

The Prayer

"Oh, mighty Father, help me. Again, I have this pain in my head. Oh, Father, every time I wake up, I swear not to get this pain in my head, and every night I go out and find it, only to bring it home with me. Oh, Father, if only you would send me some money so that I would not have to go out into the wicked town to work. Perhaps there would be one day in my life when I could stay home. If you, kind Father, would send to me some money so that I could stay home and rest my aching head, I would be so grateful."

The young man stood and crossed himself as he staggered with his hangover down the road to work.

The priest crossed himself, too.

Every morning Salomon stopped outside the church to pray his little prayer. Every morning the priest listened, and his heart was touched by this hard-working man's words. Tomorrow the priest would tie up a half dollar and drop it down to Salomon so he would have one day when his head would not hurt.

The next morning, Salomon came hobbling to the church. He held his head slightly forward the way one does when it throbs. Salomon bent his head and prayed his prayer.

The priest waited until Salomon was finished, and then carefully dropped the half dollar (all rolled up in a linen napkin) from the window above down to Salomon.

Just at that moment, Salomon lifted his head as if to say good-bye to God. The half dollar fell swiftly and landed hard on Salomon's forehead, knocking him to the ground.

The priest wanted to cry out, but knew that he should not speak. Salomon regained his composure and shook his fist up at the sky. "Thank You, God, for you only sent down a half dollar silver piece. If You had dropped a whole *dollar* silver piece, You surely would have killed me. Thank You, God!"

Salomon went on his way. Such is the way of Salomon.

The Three Sisters and Luck

The youngest of three sisters married a man who had great wealth. She invited her two older maiden sisters to come and live with her and her husband. The four of them had a good life with plenty of room in the simple four-bedroom home. All was well until the wife became pregnant. The older sisters then spent a great deal of time talking privately betweem themselves. When the wife's first child was born, her maiden sisters put a piece of flesh in the crib and threw the child out of the window into the garden. The wife was horrified to find that instead of a fine healthy baby there was a dried up piece of flesh. The wife sank into depression and cried for days. The husband was most concerned, and unsure about this predicament.

The old gardener had happened to pass by the window and had heard the muffled cry of an infant. He quickly located the baby. The gardener hurriedly took the infant to his loving woman. This infant was a blessing to him, for he and his wife had never been able to have children.

When the second child was born, the sisters replaced it with a cat. The wife was terrified and begged her sisters to tell her what had happened to the baby. The sisters clicked their tongues and responded that when they assisted with the birth, the cat was all there was.

Again, the second infant was found in the garden by the gardener.

The sisters were ever so glad to dispose of the babies, for the babies would grow and push *them* out into the cold cruel world.

One day, the husband invited all the town's small children to come to a party in his garden. The gardener asked if he might bring his children, for they would love to see the garden and the house where he worked. The husband agreed.

When the gardener's children arrived, the husband noticed a striking resemblance between the children and his wife. He asked the gardener about his children.

"Oh, they were a gift from God."

The husband pressed him further. "How do you mean?"

The gardener smiled. "All my life I have grown roses, flowers, and trees, but one day infants started to grow from the garden, the garden right under your wife's window. These children grew from the love and tending of the flowers."

The husband then knew where the children had come from, and indeed this *had* been a gift, for he also knew what had happened.

He asked the gardener and his wife to come and share their meal that evening. The husband invited the sisters to join them, also. After the meal, the husband made an announcement:

"It has been brought to my attention that this house is much too large for my wife and me. Therefore, without another day passing, I have decided to give the house to the gardener who has loyally kept the grounds all these many years and whose family is larger than our own. This man well deserves this large house for his wonderful family.

"My wife and I shall live in the gardener's house, and the rest of you will do what you must."

The gardener was dumfounded with joy. The gardener's wife was very surprised. The sisters were spitting mad and left before midnight.

The husband and his wife lived happily in the gardener's cottage. They had nine healthy children. The wife taught all the children out in the garden when the weather was good and in by the fire on the cold winter nights.

The husband—well, you can imagine, he had to work very hard for all this happiness.

The Sheepskin

Feel it, feel, feel how soft it is.
This was my mother's.
She would sit there by the fire.
She would hold it in her lap like this.
She would stroke it up and down.
She would hold it close to her bosom and laugh.
Feel how worn the back is.
This sheepskin was her first.
My father took it from their first lamb slaughtered.
He cured the skin, gave her the meat to fix for dinner, and I am sure he watched her smile.
Her smile, her smile made you feel loved.
Her smile showed her crooked white teeth, cracked from breaking piñon nuts.
Her smile wrinkled the worn brown skin of her cheeks.
Her smile lit her brown eyes to a radiant glow.
Her smile gave you love.
The sheepskin is still here, after all this time.
My brothers were washed, diapered, nursed on this sheepskin, and so was I.
My father lay his head on this sheepskin when he napped.
My mother cried on this sheepskin when he died.

My mother kneaded her fingers into it when my brothers went away.
I stayed.
I stayed and watched her smile.
Feel it, feel how soft this is.
Feel its warmth, my daughter.
Come, let me see you smile.

Postman

There was a postman who lived in Las Trampas, New Mexico. He was a good postman, and one day he got up early. He felt fine, for he had received his crisp new postal uniform. He ate his breakfast of beans and tortillas with pork, took his mailbag, and kissed his wife good-bye.

His lovely wife reminded him that his older sister from the big town of Taos was coming for dinner that evening. Every time his sister came for dinner, she brought him a present of great thoughtfulness.

The postman set off on his route. The weather was cool, and fall was in the air. The tall ponderosa pines were green, and the pristine aspen were just turning to gold. Hawks circled high above the land calling out warnings of the cold weather to come.

The postman crossed the high road and decided to take a short cut across the mountain. As he started uphill, he heard a voice call out to him, "Sir, stop, stop there!"

The postman ignored the voice, preferring to listen to the wind rustle in the trees, and continued on his route.

"Sir, I assure you that I mean to harm you if you do not stop!"

The postman walked on. He thought of turning and facing the rude speaker, but could not imagine what purpose it would serve, for certainly the voice was not referring to him.

The voice shouted out louder this time, "Sir, I am holding a gun, and you are to stop or I will shoot you!"

The postman stopped and turned. The postman asked the man who approached him,

83

"What is it you want of me?"

The man was dressed in ragged clothes. His face, dirty and unshaven, showed youth and despair. "I want you to give me that mailbag. I have watched you for some time, and I want the mailbag."

The postman listened carefully to the voice. It was not one he knew. The postman did not hand over the mailbag, but answered firmly, "I cannot give you this mailbag without a reason. Why do you want the mailbag?"

The robber lifted the gun up to the postman's face. "Give it to me, or else I will shoot you. Do you want that?"

The postman backed away from the gun. "Listen, I have never in all my years been late delivering the mail. If I cannot deliver the mail, then I would like it at least to look good."

The robber let the gun fall to his side. "What?"

The postman looked through the trees. "I will give you the mailbag if you will do me a favor." The postman had decided this man was new to the area, and perhaps new to being a robber.

The robber tilted his head to one side. "What favor? I am robbing you!"

The postman held his finger up. "Wait, if you will let me take off my jacket…"

The postman put the mailbag down on his boots and pulled off his jacket. "Here. If you shoot two holes in my jacket, one here in this sleeve and one here in the other sleeve, it will look convincing that I was held up. If I just return and say, 'Well, I was robbed,' do you think anyone will believe me? No. So please, shoot one hole here and one here."

The postman held the jacket up away from him, hoping that this robber was a good shot.

"Why two holes?" the robber asked.

The postman frowned. "I don't want to have a patch here on this side and nothing on the other. This will balance the jacket."

The robber scratched his head, and then he lifted the gun and shot two holes, one in each elbow of the postman's jacket.

The postman put the jacket on and examined the work. It was good, but then the postman clicked his teeth and shook his head.

"What's wrong now?" the robber asked.

The postman continued to shake his head. "They will just say that I left the jacket in the forest and someone shot holes in it. They will not believe that I was robbed. Here, you better shoot these."

The postman took the mailbag and leaned it against the tree. He took off his jacket and laid it on top of the mailbag. Then he sat down and took off his boots, his socks, and his pants.

The robber stood there shaking his head. "What do you want me to shoot now?"

The postman stood up in his shirt and underwear. He lifted up his pants holding them away from his body.

"Shoot here and here, just a little above the knees. Hope you can shoot without hitting me."

The robber chuckled. "I am an excellent marksman, watch this."

The robber shot two holes, evenly, one in each side of the pants legs. The postman was impressed.

The postman put his pants on, he shook out his socks and put them on, but his boots he lifted up and placed against the tree trunk.

"Just so we have things balanced, why don't you shoot a hole in the bottom of each one of my boots?"

The robber smiled. This postman was going to be cold in the fall with all the holes in his clothes. The robber lifted the gun and shot holes in each of the new black boots. The postman sat down and put on his boots. He dusted them off before he pulled them on, carefully smoothing his pants leg over each one.

The postman then stood up, saluted the robber, lifted his mailbag over his shoulder, and walked away up the trail to deliver mail to those who lived on the north side of the mountain. The robber lifted the gun in the air, aimed, and heard the gun click on an empty chamber. The robber sighed.

The day warmed as the sun rose in the sky, but by mid-afternoon the weather turned cold. The postman was not late, although he did have a nasty cough by the time he got home for dinner that evening.

He dressed in his best clothes for his sister's visit. As for his new uniform, his wife never mentioned the holes—she just mended them.

Eyes That Come Out at Night

There was a boy who was told to spend the night with an elderly neighbor woman, for his parents were out of town. The boy gathered his belongings and took them to the old woman's home. He helped her with the chores, and when the time came to go to bed, he would sleep in the living room. The old woman picked up her black cat and put it outside. She went to the alcove where she slept, just off the living room, and she pulled a curtain across the doorway.

The boy was curious. He tiptoed to the curtain. He ever so cautiously peeked at the old woman. He saw her unscrew her legs and place them under her cot. He saw the old woman scratch her brown eyes so that they fell into her hand. She put them in a round saucer on a table by her bed.

The boy went back to his bed in the living room. He tried to sleep, but the black cat kept clawing at the door and crying at the window. The boy felt sorry for the black cat, and he opened the door. The cat ran into the house, slipped under the curtain, and jumped up on the table by the old woman's cot. The cat leaned over the saucer and ate the brown eyeballs.

The boy was scared and left early in the morning to go home. A day or two later, he met the old woman on the road. Her eyes glowed a deep green. He asked her politely how she was, and she said she had a terrible headache and missed his company. He said he would help her home.

When they got to her house, she invited him in for some cake. He ate the cake, thanked the old woman, and left. Outside, he bumped into the black cat. Its eyes were sunken shut. Its eyes were gone!

The boy ran home, and never went back to the old woman's house again.

The Mule

Once upon a time, there was a poor man who was responsible for the care of the horses and the burros at the local hotel and bar. The poor man was called Pedro, and he wore rags. He chose to wear rags because his nicer clothes were such that they should not be worn in a barn while tending horses.

One day, the rich priest of the area came to the hotel bar for some refreshments and relaxation. The priest was called rich for his wealth was in the people. The people did love this kind, humble man who preached of equality among men and women, between church and state.

The rich priest rode a fine mule, a prize animal well trained to walk with a high prancing step.

The rich priest enjoyed meeting the people in the fields, drinking with them in the cafés or bars, and sharing their problems and rewards. The rich priest always rode his prize mule.

Pedro took the reins of this fine mule and led him into the barn. Pedro polished the beautiful saddle, folded the thick saddle blankets, and wiped off the silver-trimmed bridle. Pedro fed the mule and brought him fresh water. In the morning, Pedro fed the mule again. He put the handsome blankets on the mule's back. He dusted off the finely tooled saddle and placed it gently on the mule. He rubbed oats on the bit and pulled the shining bridle over the mule's head, saying, "Ah, this mule leads the life of a rich one. He has plenty of food, and wears trappings of great quality. I wish I could be in this mule's

place."

That is what he said, seeming to be actually speaking to the mule. (This habit is also known among horse owners.) This mule, as it happened, turned his head to Pedro and said, "I will *gladly* change places with you, sir. Carrying the rich priest is not easy—he is a very big man!"

Pedro looked around the barn. He walked around the mule. He studied the mule's eyes. "Are you talking to me?"

The mule winked one eye. "Yes, I am talking to you, sir. I will gladly change places with you, for you are very intent on being in my place and I have never known what it is like to be a man. Let us change."

Pedro rubbed his chin. "Yes, this is good!"

The mule lifted his front leg high in the air. Pedro took hold of his fetlock. There was a big puff of smoke, and Pedro was the mule and the mule was in Pedro's body.

Pedro stood in the barn feeling his four legs on the dry straw. He sniffed through his furry nose, sneezing from the hay dust. Pedro's head was now heavy, and his tail swatted nervously back and forth. He shook his head and tried to talk, but he only made a gurgling sound in his throat.

This sound reminded him of his wife and his mother-in-law. If he was to be the mule of the rich priest, he would be traveling all over the country, and he should in politeness say good-bye to his wife and his mother-in law.

Pedro turned to leave the barn, but he was tied to the stall gate. He pulled on the bit, which stuck hard up into the roof of his mouth. He let the reins go slack and slowly pulled at the ends with his teeth. He got them loose. Just then, the boy from the bar came into the barn

92

and took hold of the reins, leading Pedro out into the courtyard.

The rich priest was saying prayers to the people. Pedro reared back and pulled free. He cantered down the road to his home. His mother-in-law was sitting outside on the porch, busily spinning wool. Pedro wanted to touch his mother-in-law and get her blessing before he went off on his journey.

The mother-in-law looked up and saw a *mule* coming on the porch. Pedro called out for her not to be afraid. His braying terrified her, and she fell over in a faint. Pedro's wife came to the door with a large bowl of hot water and threw it on him. Some men by now had arrived from the courtyard and caught Pedro by the reins. They tried to pull him back to the barn, but he would not go.

He splayed his feet out, falling on his stomach, and he rolled over and over in the dirt. Pedro then bolted up and ran into his house and sat in his chair. The people came in and whacked him with brooms. Pedro finally gave in to their tugging on his bridle. The boy took Pedro back to the stable to clean him.

The rich priest rode Pedro for a while, and then he had to say, "Thanks be to God, this mule rides like the rolling wind."

Some people suggested that the rich priest might stand up in the stirrups. The rich priest did. It was much better. Others seeing the rich priest stand in the saddle bowed down to him. Pedro thought the people were stupid to do this, and he started to laugh. His laugh choked in his throat and he began to cough. The more Pedro coughed, the more frightened the rich priest became. The rich priest called out for help. He sat down on his haunches. The rich Pedro thought he should do something to help.

priest rolled over backwards in a somersault and landed in the dirt. This made the rich priest angry, and he jumped up and tightened the saddle girth. He scolded Pedro for sitting down in the dirt.

Pedro stood up, and the rich priest remounted.

They went on until they came to a town. Pedro watched the people come out to meet the rich priest. They were carrying a tall wooden cross. Pedro knelt down before the cross as he had been taught to do from a very young age. The priest rolled forward in a somersault and landed in the dirt.

The rich priest dusted himself off, apologized to the people for his unreliable mule, remounted, and rode to the square. There, he dismounted and led the mule to the church. Pedro stood outside and waited for the rich priest to finish the sermon.

Pedro heard a familiar voice beside him. "Pedro, I have come running to find you. I cannot live with your wife. She talks all the time about things that I do not understand. By my faith, I do not understand people or their ways."

Pedro nudged him, and said as best he could in his limited mule's voice, "I am willing to trade, for I miss my wife and my mother-in-law."

Pedro put out his nose and touched the man in his body. In a puff of smoke, they changed places again. Pedro was ever so glad to be with his wife and mother-in-law.

Pedro became very respectful of all mules after that, although he was cautious about what he said to them.

94

The Ant

An ant noticed the beauty of a spider's web. The morning dew clung to each and every thread of the web. The ant climbed up on the wooden beam of the front porch to get a better look at the beautiful lace. There, she came to a small silver door. The ant knocked on the door, and the spider opened it.

The ant said, "Spider, you have a beautiful home. You live in the most beautiful home I have ever seen."

The spider invited the ant to come in and visit. The spider showed the ant all of her storage rooms. The ant was very impressed.

"When winter comes, you will have plenty of food."

The spider was quite proud, and invited the ant to stay for dinner. The spider went into the kitchen to prepare the food. There was a knock on the door.

The ant answered the door. A grasshopper stood outside with his hands stretched out.

"Please, if you will, give me some food."

The ant went into the kitchen and asked the spider. The spider went to the door and invited the grasshopper in.

But the grasshopper would not be still. He was so excited that he jumped up and down, up and down, up and down, until he had knocked in four walls and smashed some dishes. This was very sad.

The spider told the grasshopper to leave, for he was ruining her home. The grasshopper

left empty-handed.
    Such is life.
    Good manners and polite gestures will get you far, but gathering food for the cold winter nights will get you farther still.

The Animals' Escape

There once was a mean man who lived in a house high up in the mountains between Arizona and Utah. The wife of this man had given up on finding any joy in him, and she had gone her own way back down into the valley to live a life of goodness and caring.

This man was so bitter at his inability to have full control over any *person* that he held his animals in chains. He had a big kitchen where meals were prepared for the wealthy landowners and their workers. The man took great satisfaction in charging outrageous prices for food that was prepared by animals.

He had a cat, a rooster, and a sheep. They were his slaves in the kitchen. The man never let them sleep or rest. The animals decided to escape. They planned to leave at the early light of day, for that was when the man finally sat down and fell asleep. They watched and listened for the man to begin to snore. At last they heard the soft sounds of sleep.

The rooster lifted the sharp meat knife from the high shelf. The cat held it firmly, and by sawing the heavy chains back and forth, they finally broke free of their bonds.

They gathered up some food, and instead of leaving by the front door, they chose to leave by the back door. Their trail would be harder to follow, for they would go up the mountain and come down the other side by the river. The mountain was steep in places and had many trees, streams, and valleys.

The animals were so excited about their escape that they talked loudly among themselves as they fled. A sharp bark silenced their chatter. All around them, studying them hungrily, wolves appeared. The wolves laughed at their silence.

One of the wolves called out, "We are going to eat you up, what do you think about that?"

The cat studied the wolf that spoke. "You, friend wolf, are old. You should boil us until we are soft, or else you may lose what few teeth you have left."

The wolf licked his lips. "Certainly, that is what I had in mind. Come this way."

The wolves led the animals to an clearing in the forest. There on a pile of sticks was a big cast-iron pot. The wolves lifted the animals into the pot. The younger wolves brought buckets of water and filled it up. The older wolves brought more sticks and placed them under the cast-iron pot. The wolves waited as the fire burned slowly.

All of this had taken time, and the sun was going down.

The warm, pink fingers of evening stretched out across the sky. The wolves rolled in the dirt nearby and took a small nap.

The sheep nudged the rooster. The rooster nudged the cat. The cat climbed on the sheep's head and jumped out of the pot. The rooster flew down to the fire and carefully lifted the burning sticks with his beak, throwing them to the side. The cat brought a branch to the sheep who with his delicate feet leaned on it until the pot fell over on its side.

The sheep squeezed and squeezed until he finally pushed out of the pot and stood on the dry ground. His thick wooly fur had soaked up all the water, making him so heavy he could hardly walk. The cat and the rooster ran ahead.

The sheep sloshed and groaned, moving in slow steps. The sheep finally shook himself and was able to move faster. He followed the cat and the rooster.

The wolves awoke surprised to find their dinner had escaped. They gathered, and decided to follow the wet drips on the ground.

Meanwhile, the three animal friends had come across an old house. Standing outside the house was an old ox. He welcomed them to his house, telling them of his lonely life. They sat and shared food and stories in the ox's kitchen.

The wolves were now very hungry. They had been running for some time with their noses close to the ground. As they were running, they met a coyote. The coyote laughed when he heard their story. "You caught your dinner, then let it get away? You are stupid wolves!"

The wolves stared at the coyote.

The coyote laughed and laughed, boasting, "I could catch your dinner, and I would hold onto it until it was eaten!"

The wolves grinned. "Very well then, *you* catch the cat, the rooster, and the sheep. You are so smart, Coyote, you do it."

The coyote agreed and set out in the dark of night to find the animals. He came to the ox's house and heard the animals talking. The coyote could not help himself—he started to laugh.

The cat heard the laugh. The rooster nodded that he heard it, too. The sheep shook his wet furry head, and the ox blew out the candle on the table. The coyote thought they were going to bed. He waited for a while, and then he opened the door.

As he entered the room, the cat jumped on his back, sinking all four sets of claws into him. The rooster flew up and pecked out his eyes. The coyote stumbled, falling over the wet sheep who let out a loud *baa*, which under the circumstances was quite frightening. The ox lowered his horns and lifted the coyote, throwing him out the open door, through the air, into a patch of cactus.

The coyote limped back the way he had come, and when they found him, the wolves surrounded the coyote and nipped at him for not bringing back their dinner.

The three friends live with the ox, for they still have many stories to share.

100

The Dispute

In the general store last Wednesday, three men happened to come together. They had known each other by name, but did not know each other well. One of these gentlemen, as one should respectfully acknowledge, was a doctor. Here we refer to doctors as *médicos*, men of medicine. This *médico* was new to the area. He was a public health doctor who carried around with him a "knowledgeable" attitude. The *médico* was buying some rolls of cloth, plain white cloth, perhaps for bandages.

The *médico* was behind another man who wore polished, hand-tooled leather boots and belt. This second man was the *ranchero*, the ranchman. He is given great respect as well, for besides the land he owns, he also holds all the cowboys', cooks', and maids' paychecks. The *ranchero* carried a long, coiled rope. The *ranchero* held his head high, for he had much knowledge about land, people, and power.

The *ranchero* was anxious to get back to his ranch. The man in front of the *ranchero* was taking quite a while to make up his mind. The third man was a sheepherder, a *borreguero*. *Borregueros* are very peaceful people, never hurried, rather quiet unless pushed, and they smell. Yes, they smell so strongly that it is difficult to be near them for too long, unless, of course, you are a sheep. Sheep know the smell of their *borreguero*, and so if they get separated from the flock, they sniff the wind, and they find their *borreguero* by the odor in the air.

This *borreguero* wanted to buy some licorice. He was shown the red and the black licorice, and he couldn't decide whether to take the one he knew (the black), or to try the one he had

never seen before (the red). He could not decide.

The médico shoved the ranchero to the side, yelling at the borreguero, "Make up your mind, man, and let the rest of us through!"

The ranchero, ruffled by being shoved, frowned at the médico. "Hey, you know nothing of people. The harder you push them, the more confused they will get!"

The médico retorted, "What do you know? You, the one who thinks he knows everything about people and animals, you know nothing!"

The woman behind the counter smiled. "You two know less than the borreguero. Give him his time."

That did it. The ranchero and the médico started arguing over who had the most knowledge. The borreguero stood pondering over the two candy jars of licorice. The mood was getting nasty behind him.

The woman behind the counter called out to the two arguing men, "Listen, you two, if you know so much, let us put your knowledge to a test."

The ranchero was already unrolling his rope, and the médico was pulling on his cloth. "Fine, let's put our knowledge to a test!" Both men answered in unison.

The woman smiled. "In the back, behind the store, is a shed. There is a skunk in that shed who will not leave. We have tried everything, and the skunk stays in there. The one who can get the skunk out of the shed is the one who has the most knowledge. One who can manage a skunk can surely manage anything or anyone."

A large group had gathered to see about the dispute, and this audience clapped and nodded. The two men shook hands.

"Fine, we will take the challenge. But the borreguero has to enter into the contest, too. If he wins, we will each buy him a piece of licorice."

The two men were now slapping each other on the back. The borreguero smiled.

The woman behind the counter called her daughter to mind the cash register and went outside with the men. She took a stopwatch from her apron pocket and asked, "Which one of you will go first?"

The ranchero shoved the médico forward. "He gets to go first. He is the one who is in a hurry."

The médico dusted off his suit jacket. "Sure, I will go first and get rid of the skunk, and then all of you lovely people can go home to your families."

The audience chuckled; some clapped.

The woman held the door open. The médico walked in and shut the door. The woman called aloud, "Thirty seconds, forty seconds, fifty seconds…"

The door flew open, and the médico raced past them, handing the cloth to the woman as he disappeared into the crowd.

The woman smiled at the ranchero. "All right, ranchero, it is now your turn. You go in and bring out the skunk."

The ranchero lifted his fine cowboy hat, pushed his hair back, and nodded. His confidence was strong. He unhooked the rope and handed it to the woman. She held the door for him. He walked into the shed and shut the door. The woman lifted the stopwatch. "Thirty seconds, forty seconds, fifty seconds, sixty seconds, seventy seconds…"

The door flew open, and the ranchero with hat in hand walked quickly away from the shed. His face was flushed and his forehead wet with sweat. As he walked hurriedly away, he stumbled into the médico who was standing on his toes watching from the back of the crowd.

The woman cleared her throat. "Now it is time for the borreguero."

The borreguero bowed his head, walked through the open door, and shut it firmly behind him. The woman once more lifted her hand. "Thirty seconds…"

The door flew open, and out flew the skunk, running at a speed that can only be imagined, racing for the hills behind the shed. The crowd went wild. The médico and the ranchero shook their heads.

The borreguero went home to his sheep with two pieces of licorice in his pocket, one red and one black. So much for the dispute of last Wednesday.

The Mountain Lion and the Mouse

A young brown mountain lion sat by a rain pond. He stretched forward yawning, and then he stretched back, swishing his tail and lifting his rear end high into the air. The warm sun heated the damp earth around him. Thunder and lightning had set the sky to music and lights the night before. Rain had washed away the dry dirt that had collected on every claw, every pad, and every fine, fat, soft layer of fur on his strong body.

This mountain lion turned his head just so, just enough, to see his reflection in the rain pond. He glared at his reflection staring back at him. He lifted his upper lip challenging his mirrored image to battle. Then, with a glimmer in his golden eye, he turned and flipped his tail at the poor frightened creature in the rain pond.

The mountain lion lay down under a thick juniper tree. He studied its trunk. This tree was hundreds of years old, and in all those hundreds of years, it still was just an ugly tree. The mountain lion yawned. He licked his powerful front paw, swallowing a fly in the process.

The mountain lion's contentment was interrupted by the sound of something lapping water from the rain pond.

The mountain lion gracefully turned his head. Growling a warning deep in his throat, he called out, "Who is there?"

The bobcat respectfully showed himself. "It is I, Bobcat. I have come for a drink of fresh rainwater from the rain pond." The bobcat quickly lay down on the moist dirt and rolled over, showing his stomach.

The mountain lion was not amused at his submissiveness. "Bobcat, tell me why is it that I am so strong, graceful, and majestic—and you are but a bobcat?"

The bobcat respectfully answered as he ran, "I don't know, noble Mountain Lion."

The mountain lion frowned. "Humph!" he said.

The mountain lion decided he would take a stroll. His strong legs carried him over the little rolling arroyos on top of the mesa. His perceptive ears heard a busy chattering. He turned only so slightly, for he was not one who was easily distracted—or who wished to *appear* to be easily distracted.

There on a sandy pile was a prairie dog. The prairie dog did not see the mountain lion, for he was busy chattering to someone in the other direction. The mountain lion lifted the corners of his mouth and roared, "Prairie Dog, why aren't you as handsome and powerful as I?"

The prairie dog did not wait to answer but dodged into a hole and was out of sight in a blink.

"Too honest to answer, eh?"

The mountain lion went on his way. He stopped at an overlook. The mountain lion could see a grey ribbon far below him with objects moving on it. None of those objects ever came up to his land.

Even the clouds stayed up above him. They moved with the fast wind over the mountain lion's finely shaped head. The mountain lion continued along the side of the escarpment. A lone coyote came trotting up to him.

The coyote was busy sniffing the ground and almost ran into the mighty mountain lion.

The mountain lion let a soft rumble roll out from his throat.

The coyote stopped abruptly and moved to the side. The mountain lion confronted him.

"Coyote, why aren't you powerful, muscular, and handsome like me?"

The coyote replied, "You are the most handsome, certainly, Mountain Lion. It is best."

The coyote flattened down and slunk away, hiding behind a chamisa bush.

The mountain lion shook his head, fluffing the fur along his back. His coat was smooth and glistening, and he felt stronger and more powerful today than ever. The mountain lion sat down under a ponderosa pine tree. The tall tree shaded him from the hot sun. The mountain lion yawned. His tail moved slowly up and down. He was bored.

A mouse came scurrying past him. The mountain lion lifted his big paw and placed it smack in front of the mouse.

"MOUSE!!!" the mountain lion roared at the little creature, "Mouse, why am I so strong and powerful, and you so weak and small?"

The mouse, without a moment's thought, climbed to the top of the mountain lion's paw. The mouse rubbed his ear with his tiny left paw. The mouse studied the mountain lion for some time, and then he looked down at his paws.

The mountain lion was impatient, "Well, what is your answer?"

The mouse cocked his head ever so slightly, letting his right ear droop. "I guess this hasn't been one of my better days."

The mouse scurried off, eager to be on his way.

The Dead One Fell

There once was a boy who lived with his mother and his older brother. They were very poor. Each summer they would go out in different directions looking for work.

The mother did cleaning. She was excellent at washing, mending, and wrapping clothes. The older brother was basically lazy—he got simple work such as weeding, sweeping, or washing fruit. This didn't pay very much, and he didn't seem to care. The youngest son was a hard worker, but he was very young. Not too many farmers trusted him to do a man's job.

This young boy searched for work all day, and no one took the time to try him.

The chicken farmer laughed when the young boy offered to clean out the coop. "You are so small that you would be buried in there! Go home, little fellow."

He was too short, too young, too little to know the right ways. That is what the cattleman told him. When the young boy offered to help knead bread for a farm woman, she scolded him for running away from home and threatened to pour hot water on him if he did not leave her kitchen door.

Even the sheepherder, who was known for his good temper, did not understand. The sheepherder stood and looked and looked and could not figure out where the voice was coming from, for he could not see a man.

The sun was going down, and the boy knew he would not make it home before dark. He was disappointed about his search and would feel terrible when he told his family that he couldn't find work.

The boy decided to stay out on his own. He was very hungry, but if he could not con-
tribute to the food for his family, he must continue looking for work.

He wandered down the road, and the night got darker and darker until it was pitch black.
He ran into something hard. It hurt. He felt along the side of this hard object and discovered
that it was a house. Feeling his way along, he came to a door. He fell into an empty room—and
fell asleep.

He was awakened by a strange scraping sound coming from the roof above him. He sat up,
felt for a window opening, and looked out to see nothing in the darkness. He heard a loud,
echoing voice, and tilted his head as he listened to it.

"Well, what is it now?" the voice said.

"I am going to fall. I just know that I'm going to fall," another voice answered.

"Well, fall then, and get it over with," said the first voice.

Out of the black night sky a white bone appeared. It fell through the air and landed with a
thud just outside the window where the young boy watched.

"I'm going to fall. It will be awful, but I know I am going to fall," said another voice from
above.

"Fall. Go ahead and fall," said the loud, echoing voice.

Another white bone appeared and fell down near the first one.

One by one, bones cried out in the dark. They appeared and fell, one after another. Soon
there was a whole skeleton's worth of bones lying on the ground.

The young boy gasped as he saw the bones all come together in a standing skeleton. The
skeleton clanked its way to the young boy.

"Aren't you a brave boy! Other boys would have run home. Because you are so brave, I am

111

going to beat you with my strong bones."

The young boy stood up glaring at the skeleton. "All right. You can hit me, but I will hit you back."

The skeleton fisted up his bony hand and swung at the young boy. The boy ducked and socked the skeleton hard in the ribs. The good punch hit the skeleton and threw him down on the mud floor.

"You are a strong boy. You are not only strong but also very brave." The skeleton stood up. He walked around the young boy. The boy turned, ready to fight. "You are small and young, but you are brave and strong—to say nothing of careful. Because of this, I will give you all my jewels and gold. All that I have will be yours."

The boy thought this was good luck. The skeleton gave him a candle. The skeleton magically lit the candle by blowing on it, and gave it to the boy, showing him another room. "You can go in and count the gold and silver."

The boy took the candle, and he had turned away from the skeleton to go into the room when the skeleton jumped onto his back.

"If you take my wealth, then you have to carry me."

"All right," said the boy as he walked into the room. He had stopped to focus his eyes when the skeleton leaned over his shoulder and blew out the candle.

Because this young boy was so good-tempered, he did not get angry with the skeleton. "I want to see what your riches are," he said.

The skeleton relit the candle. Just as the boy turned again to look at the gold and riches, the skeleton raised up over his shoulder and blew out the candle.

Now, the boy may have been a good-tempered boy, but this made him mad. He threw the skeleton off his back. "If you're going to keep blowing out the candle, I'm going to leave."

"No, no, please don't do that, my young, strong, brave boy. Please, please don't leave me alone. I think you are a *very* brave boy."

The boy held up the candle, and its flame sprang up again. The boy studied the room, and his eyes grew very wide, and his mouth fell open. There, along the floor and in chests, were tremendous piles of gold and silver and rubies and diamonds and beautiful jewels. He touched the wealth, held bits of it in his small hand, and let it fall—this was quite a sight for a little boy who had always been hungry.

The skeleton brushed himself off delicately and came over to the boy.

"I'm going to ask one thing of you, my little friend. After you have gathered everything, I want you to share all of this wealth with the people who have nothing. Give each of them a little bit of gold, a little bit of silver, and the rest will be for you. Only through goodness will you succeed." The skeleton left. He disappeared. All of his bones disappeared with him.

The boy picked up the biggest chest and dragged it outside. The sun was coming up. He pulled out of the house all the gold that was lying on the floor, and piled it next to the chest of jewels. As soon as the sun was up, he was surrounded by the people from the town and the neighboring farms.

The boy gave the farmer a gold plow harness. The weaver received a jeweled shuttle of silver. For the old seamstress, there was a tiara of diamonds and rubies. The priest's stable boy was given a pair of silver spurs with fine ruby studs that went over his boots. The rancher with the bad limp was given a silver bridle, a gold bracelet for his lovely daughter, and a pair of emerald earrings for his patient wife. The school teacher was given a set of brass bells with gold handles to call in the school children.

The chicken farmer graciously took a silver-handled knife, and the cattleman a silver hat band with many different jewels. The farm woman who baked bread was thankful for the silver bread bowl and matching spoons. The sheepherder was speechless upon receiving a golden staff.

The young boy shared all of this wealth, and what was left he took home to his family. He became a very rich man in spirit, friends, and stories.

Where the Stories Came From

Leaf Monster

When I was fourteen, I went with some friends to the dances at Santa Clara Pubelo. We drove through the community of Guachepangue, on the west bank of the Río Grande just south of San Juan Pueblo. The community is a mix of old Spanish culture and that of Indians who speak the Tewa language. We stopped to visit a friend's grandmother. The *abuelita* had just finished baking *biscochitos* in the wood stove, and let us taste the anise cookies while she told us a story.

The *abuelita* reminded us that animals in the mountains do talk, and that those who wish to take the time, courtesy, and heartfelt energy to listen will understand. In Guachepangue, the animals and their sense of humor are just as important as the people who live there. (We had been warned by the granddaughter of this *abuelita's* sense of humor.)

All through the story, the *abuelita* was getting up and down from her chair. She waved a wooden spoon while yelling, "Coyote, you make me crazy, *crazy*, CRAZY!" She pulled on the front of her apron as she whispered, "…and, you know, he did just that."

She told the story so well that we ate all of the *biscochitos*, and we were late getting home.

The Lizard

Dorothy Cotton was a friend that I met while going to college at the College of Santa Fe. She lived in Glencoe, New Mexico. Santa Fe was bleak to her for the Glencoe farming community was green and rich most of the year. She would tell us about the large farms with modern machinery; the good-looking farm hands with their fancy pickup trucks; the great ranches with the large herds of cattle, sheep, and racehorses. Glencoe is just outside the town of Ruidoso, which has one of New Mexico's race tracks. Dorothy's family were fruit growers. Her mother was always sending her jars of fruit jellies, jams, and fruit breads and cookies. Dorothy's was a good room to visit after mail call.

One night while we were studying for exams we started talking about families. Dorothy told us of her family and of her mother's friend who claimed to be a descendant of the original Frank B. Coe family, founders of the community of Glencoe in 1880. Dorothy loved telling us of the magic that would take place among the forests. We would all gather around on the dorm room floor, sitting on our books and listen.

She would pull back her long red hair, letting us see her freckled face and dark brown eyes.

"Magic is everywhere in this land. The magic that is here in this land can be believed almost anywhere for this magic holds great love, as all magic should. Here is a magic story that takes place high up in the secret mountains of Glencoe, New Mexico..."

The Shoes

Up in the hills around Cuyamungue, New Mexico, there lived two friends who competed with each other constantly. The priest who visited them from the Pojoaque Church would tell them over and over again that competition was not good for the soul. Do you think these two friends listened to the priest? They did not.

At service one Sunday morning, an old man drove up to the church in his Mercedes Benz car. He had on an expensive suit and brought an expensive gift. Someone remembered an old story at lunch, reminded of it by this rich man in his fancy car. The story told did more than the priest had been able to—it stopped the two friends from competing.

The Magician Flea

Señor Romero, who lives in Chilili, reminds us that *Chilili* has three eyes and three ells in it. Señor Romero mentioned that Romero has two ohs. That is not all that he has to impress upon us. Chilili holds one of the oldest place names in New Mexico records. The community was mentioned by Chauscado in 1581 and Oñate's scribe wrote about it in 1598. The Franciscans were baptizing the Indians who lived in this area as early as 1613. Señor Romero doesn't like talking about baptism, so he changed the subject to the fact that Romero is one of the oldest names on record in the state of New Mexico.

There are responsibilities with a name and a place this old; there are traditions. The traditions vary, but (he points to my nose) the magic of each family is kept secret. Magic was brought over by the Spaniards for they knew of great magic and they knew how to pass it down from family to family.

Señor Romero pulls two chairs from the kitchen outside so that we can sit and watch the sunset. His grizzly face is thin and his eyes close as he thinks of a way to begin his story. His wrinkled right hand cradles his left elbow as he waves his left hand in the air at the gnats. His suspenders are bright red over his pressed white shirt and proudly hold up his Sunday-best pants which hang over his polished black boots. The smell of burning piñon fills the air as the neighbors start their woodstoves in preparation for the evening meal.

"Ah," says señor Romero, "the sky is just right for this story."

The Two Friends

The town of Las Tablas is eight miles south of the town of Tres Piedras. The name *Las Tablas* comes from the Spanish for "boards" or "planks". At one time, Las Tablas was a thriving community of miners, lumberjacks, and ranchers. Now that industry has moved to other parts of New Mexico, Las Tablas is peaceful and quiet. The traditional families of Las Tablas will not leave the land nor the houses which took their families years to build.

Señora Anna Velarde told this story to the children at the county Headstart. She felt it was important that the circle of pre-schoolers understand the *abuelitos* who were coming to visit for lunch. Señora Velarde was all of twenty-three years of age and had a long line of grandparents herself. Her trim five-foot frame limped around the room showing the children how grandpas walk. Somehow her story helped the young children appreciate the fears of the *abuelitos* and give them respect.

Witches

Santa Fe in English means "Holy Faith." The city of Santa Fe is twenty miles east of the Rio Grande in the north central part of Santa Fe County, New Mexico. Many believe that it has a longer name and some even argue that the city is mis-named. Santa Fe was the third capital of New Spain. The first two capitals were San Juan Pueblo. Don Pedro de Peralta built his villa in Santa Fe in 1610 after Oñate decided to move the capital from San Juan Pueblo to Santa Fe. It is documented that Don Pedro de Peralta was ordered to build a capital for "the kingdom of New Mexico." Don Pedro de Peralta did as instruct-ed and built the town on the site of the deserted Tano Indian Village.

The capital remained strong until August 21, 1680. The Indian revolutionary Pope led a revolt against the Spanish and sent them fleeing. In 1692 and 1693 many Spanish families returned with the new governor, Don Diego de Vargas, who took the city without firing a single shot. He did this by stopping all the food and water that went into the city. On August 18, 1846, U.S. General Stephen W. Kearny took the city of Santa Fe from the Spanish/Westerns using a similar technique.

This story comes from *la gente*, the people of the area. Santa Fe used to have families who came and sat on the plaza after evening mass. Everyone would share stories, gossip, and news. All of the children were dressed up as well as the adults.

Now Santa Fe is full of strangers and most of *la gente* are gone. When asked where the stories came from, the old ones would say, "The stories rise up out of the streets. People walking along the alameda or going to the cafe will arrive with the strangest expression on their faces, for they heard a story as it lifted from the past in the cool evening air."

River Man

The bright yellow moon of fall illuminates the countryside at night, and people come outside and walk around visiting in the cool night air. Our neighbor señor Maes and his son the engineer were deep in debate when my husband interrupted them to ask what the problem was.

It seems that El Paso, Texas, and New Mexico had a water agreement. New Mexico was to supply river water to Texas to repay a past debt. Piping the water was the most efficient method. Señor Maes said that the piping of river water was a very bad idea—that river water needed to flow freely, not run through metal pipes. The son respectfully acknowledged his father, but then explained that the water was evaporating and being lost in the air as well as being absorbed by the land. The water had to be contained in pipes.

Señor Maes shook his head. "Texas has water. They have floods, the ocean, rain, they have enough. New Mexico needs its river water to run freely. That is a fact!"

My husband nodded in agreement. Señor Maes smiled at him. "Ahh, now here is a man who is willing to listen. Listen," he turned to his son, the engineer, "and you might learn something. This is the way of the river in New Mexico. My father taught this to me, his father to him, listen…"

Chicken Dinner

Javier Valencia liked to talk about El Mundo, New Mexico. *El mundo* means "the world." Javier Valencia was a traveler, and he knew of towns all across the Southwest. His favorite town was El Mundo, for this was a town that incorporated *the world.*

Javier was an ageless man with large sparkling brown eyes. He had a well trimmed moustache that outlined his smile and covered his wrinkles. According to Javier, El Mundo was on the Colorado–New Mexico state line. El Mundo was the timeless community where Javier claims this story originated.

But then, if you knew Javier like we know Javier, you would know what a storyteller he is! Javier's favorite meal of the day is mid-day meal. Everyone calls it something different, so I shall leave the mid-day meal as it is. Clever people impress Javier, as you will find out in this story…

The Mare

"I know a story. I would like to share it with you," her bright brown eyes sparkled. All the students sitting in the library turned away from the weekly storyteller and stared at Angela Lopez. Ms. Lopez was the second grade teacher at Atalaya School in Santa Fe. The students giggled and whispered to each other. Ms. Lopez waited to be asked to speak.

The storyteller asked her to come to the front of the group. "No, I will tell the story right here, by the children. My voice will carry from here."

Some of the fourth grade boys nodded enthusiastically. Ms. Lopez cleared her throat. "I heard this story from my professor at T.V.I. and he said it was all right to pass it on. Is it all right if I tell it?"

The storyteller nodded. Ms. Lopez stood up. She was tall enough to be seen over the older kids sitting in the back row, if you sat up very straight. She pushed back her shoulder length brown hair and began…

Owl Wishes

Sharon Gutierrez helped me carry the notebooks, cameras, measuring tapes, and compass back to the main camp. We had documented the last of four petroglyphs sites along the Comanche Gap area. Sharon was quiet as we walked back to the van. As I loaded the canteens, she leaned on the side on the van and began to pull on her long brown hair. "Teresa, do you think you could help me out this afternoon?"

I studied her face. Sharon was only nineteen and her ability to hide her feelings had not fully developed. She was half smiling and half frowning.

"What's going on this afternoon?" Both of us had commitments.

"Well, my father wanted to know if we could go by Starvation Peak and ask a man about some pigs."

"They have pigs at Starvation Peak?" I couldn't help myself.

"Yes, a farmer there wants to trade with my father, but my father works all week and he thought since we were all the way over here anyway we could drive by and take a look at the pigs. And since you raised pigs on your farm, you would know if they were good pigs or just pigs."

I had to smile at that. No pig is just a pig.

We drove south of Santa Fe towards Las Vegas, New Mexico. Starvation Peak is near Bernal about fifteen miles southwest of Las Vegas on the old Santa Fe Trail. It is said that a hundred and some Spanish colonists hid on top of this peak from raiding Indians. The Indians saw the people and surrounded the area. The people were forced to starve to death. At the base of this peak there is a large Spanish cross, and at night it is lit up with a highway light of some kind.

We found the turn and within minutes we were at the farm house. The pigs were fat, healthy, and kept in a cleanly swept barn. As we stood in the barn and looked up at the loft we could see a large hand-carved wooden bird cage hanging from one of the beams. The cage door was wired open. The farmer smiled when he saw us pointing it out, for he had a story…

Leticia's Turtle

María Eloisa Romero stood at the front window of the Piggly Wiggly. She was very put out at the young man who had promised her a ride home. He had picked her up promptly enough from her home in El Macho, but now where was he? María Eloisa Romero is all of her name. She stands five feet five and is not plump, but she is not thin either. Her house dress is neatly covered by her pinned apron. María Eloisa Romero is one who commands respect. She always is on time, she never forgets a birthday, and she is most appreciative of a good deed. María Eloisa Romero is married to a man that I have never met, for he doesn't come into town.

Señor Romero stays home. The Romeros live in the community of El Macho which means the "mule" or "male animal" in English. Señor Romero works very hard raising animals and selling them so that his lovely wife can go into town for supplies and gifts.

María Eloisa Romero had asked me to take her home from Santa Fe if the young man was late. He was very late. Instead of agreeing to going home right away, she decided to wait at least an hour, to be courteous of his good intentions.

This was the perfect time to tell a story, except there was no place to sit and all the people going in and out disrupted her concentration.

The A.G. truck arrived, and the men unloaded dog food bags in stacks in front of the store. They were a perfect place to sit and wait. I helped her carry her grocery sacks to the dog food and we lined them all up neatly. María Eloisa Romero politely situated herself on a fifty-pound bag of Gravy Train. She pressed her apron down firmly on her lap with her hands and began her story....

The young man arrived just in time to hear the story end. María Eloisa Romero was right. He was a very thoughtful young man.

Wise Stones

The land is rough in many places around the world, as it is in the Southwest. There are lands in Nambe, New Mexico, that within an acre have every kind of soil imaginable.

Señor Ortiz knew of the land in Nambe and he knew about people as well for he was the father of many children. Señor Ortiz had a way about him of explaining a solution through a story. The listener then had the opportunity to later come back and say, "You know, I bet we could try that and it just might work!"

Nambe is a rural settlement near the Pueblo of Nambe. It was called "Namba" by the first settlers and then "Nambayongwee" by the Tewa Indians, which means "the people from the roundish earth." Nambe was given a land grant deed by the U.S. Surveyor General of the Territory of New Mexico on September 29, 1856. It granted that the land one league from each corner of the Nambe church belonged to the Pueblo Indians. This made life easier for the people.

Señor Ortiz taught me at an early age that life is basically what you make of it...

Meadowlark

Our neighbor in San Juan was señor Trujillo. He loved stories. He had the habit of getting up from his chili fields when he saw someone coming. He would walk over to them in a 'by-the-way' fashion and if the person stopped for a moment, his story would grab them. Señor Trujillo's stories covered a wide range of feelings.

Señor Trujillo told this story to my father and me on one hot August afternoon. My father and I were out looking for our puppy. Señor Trujillo was equally concerned about our puppy, for he was known to eat chilis and go back for more. (I can't remember if that was true or a story that my father told.)

Perhaps señor Trujillo stopped us on this particular day, for he had a soulful problem to work out. He never said. Somehow in all the years that I have been sharing this story of his, the reactions are different with different folks. Señor Trujillo died years ago, but his story lives on…

The Wooden Horse

Each Tuesday my five-year-old daughter and I used to take our big dogs for a walk up the mountain by our home. We would walk along a stream until we came to a dirt road. This road led us up a steep incline, through the open forest land, and to an overlook. The views in New Mexico open up to the horizon, going past the mesas, the rivers, the canyons, until one can almost believe one sees the ocean. This was our favorite place to share.

Our dogs did not find the view interesting, but they did like señor Gregorio José Jesús de Avila Atencio's garden. No matter how we tried, the dogs usually got away from us and raced for the garden. They were our calling cards. Within minutes after our arrival at the overlook we would hear señor Atencio calling the dogs. Then they would all come down the road to meet us at the overlook.

Señor Atencio was thirty-six years old the last time we met. He was a strong well-built man of six feet. His eyes were a dark green. He had blonde-brown hair that was very straight and continually fell into his face. He wore a scarf around his neck, usually a red bandana, and I never saw him in bluejeans. He wore khaki pants. His black engineer boots were always polished.

His large hands would lift my daughter up into the air and plant her firmly on his hip. "Come, it is time for some cookies." He would lead the way up the road to his two-story flat-roofed adobe home.

Señora Atencio baked. She baked cakes, cookies, pies, breads, and anything one could ever want to eat. She was a small woman of five feet and was always working. Her petite frame was highlighted by her beautiful face with her perfectly arched nose. Señora Atencio would smile and say, "Oh, there you are. We have been thinking of you." Then the plates of cookies would be put on the long wooden table. Big chairs with leather seats and backs would be pulled out, pillows found for my daughter to sit on, and baked goods passed around.

The Atencios had four boys who worked for a neighbor. We never really met the boys on a social level. They would just pass through the kitchen, grab something to eat, and be on their way.

Señor Gregorio José Jesús de Avila Atencio had a great gift for sharing stories. He was raised in Chimayo by his grandparents and this story, I have always felt, came from his life. Señor Atencio made tables, chairs, desks, beds, and doors, and he carved large animals out of wood.

The family had gardens of corn, squash, beets, and the like. The lower pastures by the house were of alfalfa and timothy grass, but they didn't have any animals.

This is Señor Gregorio José Jesús de Avila Atencio's story...

The River

María Luján was killed in a car accident about ten years ago. She was a fragile, beautiful young mother of four children. The man she was riding with was very drunk and did not stay on his side of the road.

María and I had once shared babysitters in Santa Fe. She was raised up north and missed the closeness of the people. One afternoon we had arrived at the same time to pick up our young daughters and the babysitter still had them playing in the park. We took the time to get acquainted and share family histories. She told me this story in the spring and by fall she had joined her mother and father. Her life was a hard one. Her love for life was strong. She left her story and it is not forgotten even though it still hurts to tell it...

The Flea

Stories are said to illuminate the character of the people in a particular area, and this one does that very well. It encompasses the poor sheepherders who are kind and patient, as well as the rich landowners, who have their own testings to live through.

When we were in Chimayo to help with the chili *ristras*, an old friend came over to the children and decided that they might work a bit faster if they had a story to help them along. Stories make work pleasurable.

Señor Jaramillo is one of the handsomest men in all of New Mexico. He is about six feet two, and slender, and has chocolate brown eyes which melt your soul. His family is one of the oldest in the Chimayo area and all of his children carry on the tradition of beauty and good humor.

Señor Jaramillo's concern about the children was not only that they not be bored, but that they prepare the chilis well—for señor Jaramillo not only loves to tell stories, but he loves to cook. He knelt down on the portal floor next to the children. He wiped his moustache back from his lips, studied each child's face, and began this wondrous story.

Remember

Can you remember when you were three years old?

Can you remember when you were ten?

Can you remember when you were twenty-five?

Can you remember when you were one hundred and four?

There was a dancing grandmother in San Juan Pueblo who played the harmonica. She loved to play and dance at the same time wearing her high-buttoned black shoes. She was from the old country and had come miles, over years, to marry an Indian man. She thought it was remarkable that he was sent away to school as a child, then was sent away again to college as an adult, and somehow he managed to return home only to marry a woman who had come all the way from Spain. She laughed about him, she laughed about their love, she laughed about life. She couldn't laugh and play the harmonica at the same time. This is her story about her husband the way she remembered it. But don't ask him.

The Prayer

Policarpo was a close friend of my family's. Policarpo knew just about everyone in Alcalde, New Mexico. Policarpo was my oldest brother's age and had a way with words. He liked to tell fun stories to make people laugh. This is one of those stories that once you hear it you just have to share it over and over and over again.

The power of prayer is very strong. One can pray with all of one's heart and the prayer might come true. However, if one prays and prays and does not wish it from within their heart in pure thought and feeling, the prayer will not happen.

The Three Daughters and Luck

Española is a busy town filled with low-riders, high-riders, fast food places, stores, and traders who park along the side of the road selling flagstone, vegas, firewood, and sheep. I was born in Española and find the town a treasure of stories. *Española* means "Spanish lady." No one is too sure who this particular Spanish lady was, although there is mention of a man named Juan de Jesús Naranho who arrived in the middle of the nineteenth century with a woman (no one knows if she was his wife or not) named María Juan Duran. Española is a town where the unexplainable can happen and this story comes from this most unusual and unique town.

Fate plays games on all of us, and in this story fate twists life into a better place.

The Sheepskin

Violeta María García de Trujillo was a kind, generous, loving woman who lived near the village of Velarde which is just north of San Juan Pueblo. Violeta María García de Trujillo had a voice as lovely as the robin, as soft as the dew, and as rich as honeysuckle. Everything she did contained a quality I have not found anywhere else. Violeta María García de Trujillo once picked the bitterest of gooseberries and made the sweetest gooseberry jam you ever tasted.

Violeta María García de Trujillo wore her hair in braids that were wrapped round and round her head. She wore no make-up except for Sunday lipstick. Violeta María García de Trujillo always wore a dress with a paisley print accompanied by the darkest, most wrinkled cotton support hose imaginable. Her shoes were brown with no decoration, except on Sunday, when she wore her shiny black pumps. Violeta María García de Trujillo always, but always, wore an apron. She had two aprons that I remember. One was a solid blue denim that had been washed so many times it was almost white and the other was a yellow one with lace around the collar. Violeta María García de Trujillo had two sons who were in the Navy. I never knew nor asked about her husband, and he was not around.

Violeta María García de Trujillo told me about the sheepskin that lay on her rocking chair. She was most fond of the sheepskin and this is her story…

To touch is to feel, to feel is to know, to know is to be. That is the way of the words and this is the way of the story…

Postman

The hills of north central New Mexico hold great beauty. The beauty and openness of the land give a strength to the people, the understanding of unity. The towns are close together in proximity. That is to say, the town of Ojo Sarco is about eleven miles from Las Trampas. There is one postman for each area. Each town holds a post office and a church. The people live all over the mountains of this majestically forested land.

This story was told to me by a young high school student who was warning me about the robbers and thieves in the area. His main interest was in getting a ride down the mountain to Española so that he could be with his girlfriend. He felt there was great danger in my driving alone through Las Trampas, Ojo Sarco, Las Truchas, and Chimayo to Española. There were so many strangers roaming around that one could never be too careful.

The story was worth the ride, and certainly you should know it, just in case…

Eyes That Come Out at Night

Witches are important to life in New Mexico. Witches keep everyone vigilant. This story is told in many different forms, but this is my favorite. It came from a young man who sat with my two daughters and me at the eye doctor's office. The young man was about twenty years old, and was suffering from terrible headaches. His mother said it was his eyes—she was sure he needed glasses. The young man told us the reason he had headaches was his mother's television blaring all hours of the night and day. He had come to have his eyes checked. His eyes were were dark brown, and outlined with dark curly eyelashes. His strong hands molded the story as he told it.

The Mule

Las Cruces, New Mexico, is a five hour drive south of our home. Las Cruces is a town on the border of New Mexico and Texas and just an hour or so away from the country of Mexico. It is a favorite place to visit and meet friends in the winter, for it is warm and sunny while up north the cold winds bring snow.

Las Cruces is also the county seat for Doña Ana County, which incorporates many European families. Spanish stories and Mexican stories are intertwined in this border town.

On one occasion, we decided not to drive to Mexico but to take a taxi. My husband had driven far already, and he was tired. I had my hands full with the new baby and the three year old. The taxi driver was an energetic young man of nineteen. He was most helpful with the baby, for he explained he was soon to become a father himself. My husband told him that he should save his energy—babies, he said, are totally demanding.

Once we arrived in Mexico, our three year old was asleep on my lap. The taxi driver said there was no problem. He would stay with her until we returned. My husband knew this was his cue to take the baby and leave me to ask for stories.

The taxi driver helped my husband get the stroller out and the baby settled in it. He helped him get the diaper bag over his shoulder, and he pointed to the *mercados*, the markets, that would have the best buys. My husband waved and courageously went forth.

The taxi driver then leaned through the window and asked if I wanted an ice cream.

"No, but I would like to hear a story."

Ah, his face brightened, illuminated by a smile, and he opened the passenger door of the front seat and sat down facing me. His shirt had once been white and now showed the colors of life. The richness of his story reminded me that the wealth of the soul surpasses the wealth of the pocket. This is the taxi driver's story.

The Ant

The summer was at least over and the cool evening air brought relief to the small community of Lyden, New Mexico. Aunts and uncles invited family up to help pick the fruit from the orchards around their homes. My husband and I gathered up the children and joined in the celebration of harvest. Our adopted uncle lived on the edge of Lyden and had a five-acre orchard. He lived for harvest, with all of his family there singing, picking fruit, loading up the bushel baskets in the trucks, and sharing their lives with him.

There were so many working that often a little one would be overlooked, and would stand, watching, not knowing what to do. That was when Uncle Tito would take his break. He would grab up the little one, find some shade, and tell a story. This story was his favorite, for no matter who heard it, a troublemaker or a shy mouse, the point was made.

125

The Animals' Escape

Chama is a Spanish community north of Española. Chama is very cold in the winter and can get humid and hot in the summer. The forests are tall pines. "The Animals' Escape" is an old Spanish story we heard told by a shopkeeper just off the main road. The señor was in his late fifties, a stocky man with warm brown eyes.

This señor had four dogs in the store. The oldest dog slept under the woodstove toward the back of the store. The other three dogs could be found most anywhere except behind the meat counter. The two cats, one orange striped and the other a gray tiger, sat or slept on the counter next to the cash register. We thought that perhaps these animals were as important to the store as the store owner himself.

Another man in the store was complaining about the stupidity of animals, and this story was the señor's response.

The Dispute

In northern New Mexico, people from different backgrounds, with different levels of education, share in the life of the communities. In small towns such as Tierra Amarilla or Tres Piedras, you can drive through the center of the town and wonder how it thrives. And they do thrive, for all the land around them is filled with life. The women are busy with endless chores and the telling of tales. The men work hard in the fields. The children work hard at school, play hard, and live hard.

Señora Gabaldon works perhaps a little harder than most others, and that may be because her señor works a little less. Señora Gabaldon has her hands full all the time with seven children, four pigs, twelve cows, three horses, and the running of the Post Office. She is most efficient. Señor Gabaldon can irrigate the same field for one week, whether or not there is ditch water. He thoroughly enjoys his life, and when you are around him, you enjoy his life, too. Perhaps that is why their marriage works.

This story—or "truth," as señor Gabaldon insists—actually happened down at the store in Peñasco. Each time he tells this story, it always happened last Wednesday. Wednesdays, I would say, are not a good day to go to the Peñasco General Store.

The Mountain Lion and the Mouse

The high black flat-topped mesas of the Southwest may look barren and dry, but if one were to climb to the top, she would find lush green trees and shrubs fed from rain-filled natural ponds. The wildlife is rich on top of the mesas, which are a world of their own. The steep cliffs keep out those who are not adventurous, those who do not appreciate the magic of hidden beauty.

My middle older brother reread the notice tacked on the gas station's front window. "One hundred dollar reward for a mountain lion, dead or alive."

He scratched his head. "You know, if I had that one hundred dollars, I could get me a car of some kind. What do you think?" His eighteen-year-old face was hopeful.

There wasn't any reason for me to answer, for at that time I was ten years old, and he had very little interest in what I thought. The attendant came out of the busy Española gas station building.

"That will be nine dollars."

My brother shook his head. "You are stealing. I remember when gas was only fifty cents a gallon. How come you raised your prices?"

The gas station man smiled. "Hey, if you need the money, go find a mountain lion."

That night, Papá invited some friends over for dinner. Mamá was cooking up a dinner fit for royalty when my brother mentioned hunting for mountain lions. The man who was talking with Papá immediately turned his attention to my brother.

"What is it that you said? You are going to shoot a mountain lion?"

My brother winced at the loudness of the guest's voice. "Yes, it pays one hundred dollars."

The man rubbed his chin and walked over to my brother. "One hundred dollars, eh? Well, if you kill a mountain lion, you'll put the whole of the animal kingdom in jeopardy. You know that, don't you?" My brother stared down at his size thirteen sneakers. "Excuse me, Doctor, but I think that it is time I shared a story with your son here."

The man told the story, and, you know, when he was finished, we didn't know any more than we had when he started.

The Dead One Fell

This story, about the belief that "good things come to people who do and pray for good things," comes from the area around Chupadera, New Mexico. The little boy befriends the lonely Dead One, and the Dead One gives him a reward for his courage. Perhaps in a small village of limited economy, with harsh winters and hot summers, this story is one of hope for the young boys growing up. "The Dead One Fell" is a favorite story wherever it is told, and there is always a strong, brave boy or girl in the audience to help with the telling.

OTHER BOOKS OF INTEREST FROM AUGUST HOUSE PUBLISHERS

The Oral Tradition of the American West

Adventure, courtship, family, and place in traditional recitation.

ISBN 0-87483-150-4, HB, $23.55
ISBN 0-87483-124-5, TBP, $11.95

Favorite Scary Stories of American Children

23 creepy tales, newly collected from children aged 5-10.

ISBN 0-87483-119-9, TPB, $8.95

Classic American Ghost Stories

Two hundred years of ghost lore from the Great Plains, New England, the South and the Pacific Northwest.

ISBN 0-87483-115-6, HB, $16.95
ISBN 0-87483-118-0, TPB, $9.95

Ghost Stories from the American South

More than one hundred tales of the supernatural, drawn from Tidewater Virginia to the Lone Star State.

ISBN 0-935304-84-3, TPB, $7.95

Cowboy Folk Humor

Jokes, tall tales, and anecdotes about cowboys, their pranks, their foibles, and their times.

ISBN 0-87483-104-0, TPB, $8.95

August House Publishers, P.O. Box 3223, Little Rock, AR 72203

1-800-284-8784